WAR & WARFARE

PAUL TURNER

You're History

United Kingdom: Folens Publishers, Waterslade House, Thame Road, Haddenham, Buckinghamshire HP17 8NT.
Email: folens@folens.com

Ireland: Folens Publishers, Greenhills Road, Tallaght, Dublin 24.
Email: info@folens.ie

Editor: Dawn Booth
Page design and layout: Redmoor Design, Tavistock, Devon
Picture researchers: Dawn Booth and Sue Sharp
Illustrations: Ian Heard, Nick Hawken
Cover design: Jump To!

First published 2009 by Folens Limited.
Every effort has been made to contact copyright holders of material used in this publication. If any copyright holder has been overlooked, we should be pleased to make the necessary arrangements.
British Library Cataloguing in Publication Data. A catalogue record for this publication is available from the British Library.
ISBN 978-1-85008-353-5

War & Warfare
Contents

Time terms

Time is an interesting concept. It is only because we have clocks that we can measure it passing by. Many people find it difficult to remember dates and to understand some of the terms used when discussing time. If this is a good description of you, perhaps this page will help.

Week: 7 days.

Month: 28 days during February (or 29 days in a leap year). 30 or 31 days in the remaining months.

Year: 365 days, or 366 days in a leap year.

Decade: 10 years.

Century: 100 years.

Millennium: 1,000 years.

Centuries

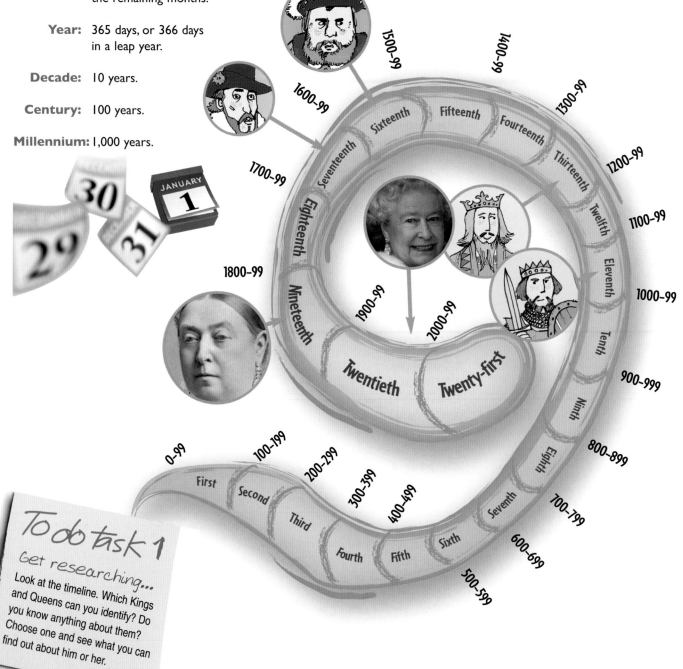

To do task 1

Get researching...

Look at the timeline. Which Kings and Queens can you identify? Do you know anything about them? Choose one and see what you can find out about him or her.

Introduction

Just when were the Middle Ages? Well, historians usually refer to the period between 1154 and 1485 as the Middle Ages. However, if we include the Norman Conquest, which was a significant turning point, the Middle Ages lasted from 1066 to 1485.

Who ruled ?

The Normans

1066–87	William the Conqueror (William I)
1087–1100	William II
1100–35	Henry I
1135–54	Stephen

The Plantagenets

1154–89	Henry II
1189–99	Richard I
1199–1216	John
1216–72	Henry III
1272–1307	Edward I
1307–27	Edward II
1327–77	Edward III
1377–99	Richard II

House of Lancaster

1399–1413	Henry IV
1413–22	Henry V
1422–61	Henry VI

House of York

1461–83	Edward IV
1483	Edward V
1483–85	Richard III

But this book isn't only about kings and queens, it's about battles and warfare. So read on and find out what it was like to fight in the Middle Ages alongside, or for, these great monarchs.

1066 is a famous date in English history. It marks the beginning of the Norman Conquest, which you may know a little about already.

- Why was the issue of the claim to the throne in 1066 so important?
  - Why did so many people believe that they had a claim to it?
  - Who was likely to win?

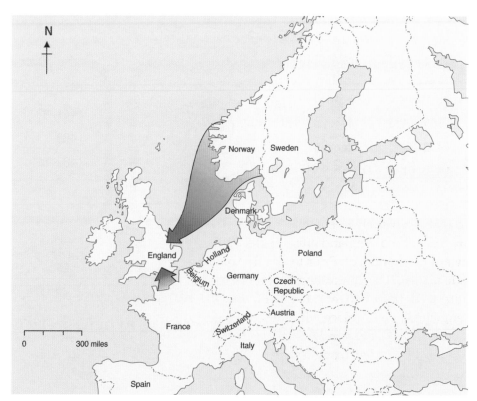

To do task 1
Comprehension
1. Who had died leading up to the battle for the English throne?
2. How was William of Normandy related to Edward the Confessor?
3. Why did Harold Godwinson have a strong claim to the throne?

Whose throne is it anyway?

In 1066 there was a problem regarding who should be the next King of England. As with any argument, all those involved believed that they were right. Yet each had an equally dubious **claim** to the throne and each was willing to fight for it. The problem arose when the previous King, Edward the Confessor, died without children; it was unclear who should succeed him even though Edward had approinted Harold to be King on his death bed

The claimants came from England, France and Norway. Can you work out how far they travelled?

N

Norway Sweden

Denmark

England Holland Poland
Belgium
Germany Czech
Republic
Austria
France Switzerland
Italy
Spain

0   300 miles

6

The main candidates for the throne were:

William of Normandy

William was a major **contender** for the throne, despite his unfortunate nickname of 'William the Bastard', which he gained due to his **illegitimate** birth – although some people would say that he earned it in many other ways. William was born in 1028 in France, and was known for dealing harshly and ruthlessly with anyone who crossed his path. As a highly experienced **campaigner**, who also commanded the respect and backing of the Pope and nobility, he believed that the throne of England would be his. He even said that he had been promised the throne by Edward (a distant cousin) in 1051 and that Harold of Wessex, another claimant, would support him.

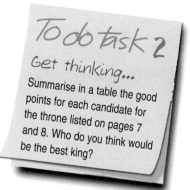

To do task 2

Get thinking...

Summarise in a table the good points for each candidate for the throne listed on pages 7 and 8. Who do you think would be the best king?

Claimant 1: William of Normandy.

Harald Hardrada

Harald Hardrada's real name was Harald Sigurdsson, but he became known as Hardrada (Norwegian for 'Hard Ruler') because of the way that he ruled. His claim lay in the fact that he was related to a previous ruler of England, King Hardicanute (1040–42) who was the son of another King of England, King Cnut. Both these kings were Danish and therefore known as Vikings. Because of this, Hardrada's plan was to use York as the base for his **invasion**, as it had a long connection with the Vikings. In a confident mood, Hardrada landed in Yorkshire ready to begin his campaign in September 1066.

BUZZ WORDZZ

Campaigner
Claim
Contender
Crowned
Embarkation
Illegitimate

A stained glass window showing claimant 2, the Norwegian, Harold Hardrada.

Harold of Wessex

Harold of Wessex was also known as Harold Godwinson. His claim to the throne was a strong one, given that he had actually been **crowned** King of England after the death of Edward the Confessor. Prior to this, Harold had made his name by controlling England's military might for Edward. His claim was also strengthened by his place within the most powerful noble family in England. He had three brothers called Tostig (see page 8), Gyrth and Leofwine.

To do task 3

Quick challenge

Look at the map page 6. How far did William and Harald have to travel to England?

Claimant 3: Harold of Wessex.

Tostig

Has anybody seen this man? The often forgotten claimant 4: Tostig.

Tostig, the brother of Harold Godwinson, was the least likely to gain the throne of England, despite having a reasonable claim. Tostig had led a troubled life. He had been stripped of the title the 'Earl of Northumberland' due to the heavy-handed way that he ruled and had effectively been exiled from England. His aim was to join up with another invading army and exploit their joint power for his own gains.

William of Normandy is on his way!

The major threat to Harold of Wessex's claim to the throne was William of Normandy: a man with a fierce reputation.

Before he could pose any real problems for Harold, however, he had to cross the English Channel by boat, which was not easy. It took William a considerable amount of time to get ready for the invasion – 9 months in total – while he built 500 boats and assembled 8,000 men and their horses for the journey to England.

Discussion POINT ?

Tostig was unlucky enough to have a more successful sibling. Can you think of anybody else in history who had the same misfortune?

To do task 4

Source work

How useful to a historian is the 'comical' Source A and why?

To do task 5

Get thinking...

Imagine you are Edward the Confessor and you are writing your will.

Who would you leave the throne to and why?

Source A — An Utterly Impartial History of Britain,
John O'Farrell, Black Swan, 2008

"Finally, after months of waiting, the wind was in the right direction. The ferry organisers apologised once again for the delay and asked customers to make their way to the **embarkation** points. Several thousand Norman, Breton and Flemish soldiers boarded for England with weapons, armour, siege equipment and horses. Any weight limit on personal baggage allowance was overlooked."

Crossing the English Channel today is slightly easier than it was in 1066, with a number of options available to people. The ferry, hovercraft and Channel Tunnel all offer speedy transportation. If you are very daring, you could even swim!

World Link

After what must have been a rough and uncomfortable crossing, William and his troops pulled their boats ashore at Pevensey on 28 September 1066. Once the troops had disembarked, William sent his boats back home to pick up supplies for what he hoped would be a long stay.

To do task 6
Use your imagination...

What qualities would a King need? Would you trust somebody who took the throne by force?

Discussion POINT ?

Has going to war got harder or easier in the last 1,000 years?

9

The Battles of Fulford and Stamford Bridge may not be as famous as the Battle of Hastings, but they saw the demise of two of the main claimants to the throne: Hardrada and Tostig.

- What impact did the Battles of Fulford and Stamford Bridge have on the question of succession?
  - For which claimants to the throne were these the end of the line?

Background to the battles

Before Harold could face William, he had the other claimants to deal with. His part in the fighting, however, did not begin until the Battle of Stamford Bridge. The early part of the conflict was entrusted to the northern Earls of England, who fought on his behalf.

The Battle of Fulford

The Battle of Fulford took place on 20 September 1066. It was fought between Hardrada, the Viking claimant to the throne who had now teamed up with Tostig, and two Anglo-Saxon Earls named Edwin and Morcar. Hardrada's army was huge, possibly numbering around 10,000. The two armies met close to the River Ouse on marshy, flat ground. The fighting was fierce and the English army was brushed aside, with many men losing their lives. However, the victorious Norwegian invasion force also suffered substantial losses, which had a knock-on effect for later campaigns. Their fierce leader was still alive, but his confidence had taken a blow.

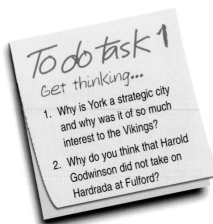

To do task 1

Get thinking...

1. Why is York a strategic city and why was it of so much interest to the Vikings?
2. Why do you think that Harold Godwinson did not take on Hardrada at Fulford?

To do task 2

Comprehension

1. When was the Battle of Fulford?
2. What rivers are close to Fulford?
3. How were the Vikings taken by surprise?

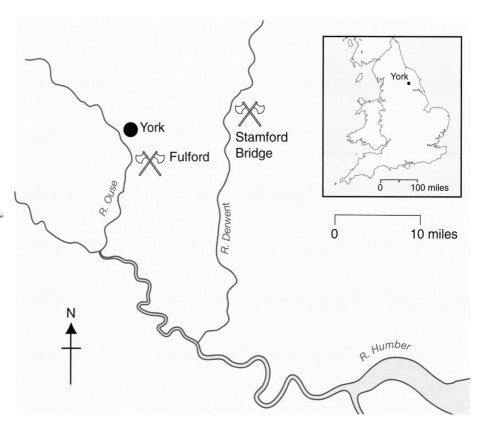

Two of Yorkshire's most notable rivers, the Ouse and the Humber, run through many miles of Yorkshire countryside, with the Humber an important tidal waterway.

The Battle of Stamford Bridge

Weakened by its victory at Fulford, the Norwegian army took an opportunity to relax by removing its armour and waiting for contact with the English. It did so close to York, at Stamford Bridge, near the River Derwent, where it was hoped that an exchange of prisoners might occur. It was a hot day and the Vikings weren't expecting conflict. This meant that they were taken by surprise by the English army, led by Harold, which came into view on 25 September 1066 (having travelled almost 186 miles over the last four days). Both sides fought fiercely, but the English were eventually victorious.

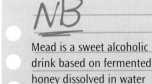

NB

Mead is a sweet alcoholic drink based on fermented honey dissolved in water and flavoured with spices.

Source A — History Without the Boring Bits,
Ian Crofton, Quercus Publishing, 2007

"*At the battle of Stamford Bridge, a single Norwegian held the bridge, holding back the English army, 'felling more than forty Englishmen with his trusty axe' – according to Henry of Huntingdon, the 12th century chronicler. Henry continued: 'At length someone came up in a boat and through the openings of the bridge struck him in the private parts with a spear.'*"

Hardrada and Tostig were both killed in the battle. The English celebrated their victory in a traditional way – with a feast of roast suckling pig and jugs of mead, among other succulent delicacies.

Source B

Battle of Stamford Bridge,
from the Battlefield Trust website

"*Agreements had been reached for hostages to be handed over to Hardrada at Stamford Bridge, some seven miles to the east of York. Hardrada, perhaps suspecting that Harold would not leave southern England under the threat of Norman invasion, felt confident enough to leave a third of his troops and armour at their base camp at Riccall, on the River Ouse, before approaching Stamford Bridge. Harold's army, probably all mounted troops, reached York on the morning of the 25th. Reinforced by the remnants of Morcar's and Edwin's forces he immediately marched from the city to Stamford Bridge, taking the Viking invaders completely by surprise.*

The battle of Stamford Bridge was a decisive victory for the English King. It proved him to be an able commander and the English troops, particularly the Housecarls, to be well trained, highly skilled and capable of great endurance. Yet in English history the victory at Stamford Bridge is inextricably linked to Harold's defeat at the Battle of Hastings, which took place less than three weeks later. Had Harold not been forced to leave William's landing on the south coast unopposed, and then face him with an army that had probably suffered significant losses, was ill-prepared and weary, then the outcome may have been very different."

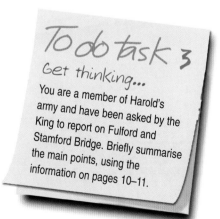

To do task 3

Get thinking...

You are a member of Harold's army and have been asked by the King to report on Fulford and Stamford Bridge. Briefly summarise the main points, using the information on pages 10–11.

Finally the two main contenders for the throne, Harold and William, met at Hastings, ready to fight it out to the death.

- Who won and why?
  - How were the English deceived by the Normans?
  - What course did the battle take?

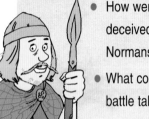

William's coming, lock your doors!

When William landed in England, his target was London: the capital and centre of power. To get there he had to travel up the country from the south coast, inevitably taking on the might of Harold's army along the way. As any good geography student will know, York is in the north of England and London is in the south so, still tired and reeling from the earlier battles, Harold's army was forced to march from the North of England to meet William's troops: a distance of 250 miles. This distance alone would have delayed Harold's progress, but he also needed to pick up more troops along the way and **rendezvous** with others at the battle ground itself. When the two forces finally came face to face, some of Harold's troops were still on their way.

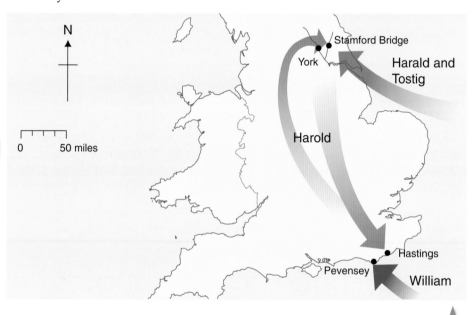

Just how much walking Harold's men had to do is clear from the map above.

To do task 1

Comprehension

1. How far did Harold's troops have to march to meet William?
2. How many troops did William have in total?
3. Who were the Fyrd?
4. What weapon did the Housecarls use?
5. What were Harold's brothers called?

That's not fair; he's got more men than us!

Harold's weary army now faced a considerable disadvantage in that they were massively outnumbered. After recruiting mercenaries from other European countries, William had around 15,000 troops at his disposal, including **cavalry** (soldiers on horseback) and 8,500 infantry (foot soldiers). The English had only 5,000 troops.

William's army, despite popular belief, was not only made up from Norman troops. It also contained fierce warriors of Breton and Flemish origin, with a few Germans and Italians. This multi-national army was heavily armed with lances, swords and bows.

Harold's army was made up from the **Fyrd**, local amateur soldiers who were armed with a mixture of makeshift weapons, and the **Housecarls**, professional soldiers who were armed with huge two-handed battle axes. There was also a considerable number of archers, who were protected by shields.

The English made their base using the advantage of higher ground. This would slightly turn the odds in their favour, despite the huge disadvantage that the small size of their army presented. They based themselves at Caldbec Hill and, before the battle was to begin, they planned to move along the prominent ridge onto Senlac Hill. Either side of this ridge was marshy ground, which would make it very difficult for the Normans to cross. William's troops were positioned at the bottom of the hill, looking up at the English.

Kick-off at 09:30

When the fighting began at around 9:30am, trumpets blared to signal the start and both armies screamed in unison as missiles littered the battlefield. The noise was horrendous as shrill shrieks and shouts echoed across the countryside. Cries of pain and anguish rang out as people began to fall on both sides.

To do task 2

Get thinking...

Imagine that you have been asked to analyse why Harold's smaller army was able to hold off William's larger army. What do you think helped Harold?

Battle of Hastings to be Hollywood film

"A £67 million US blockbuster is being planned, with the working title 'William the Conqueror'.

Producer Pamela Koffler said: 'I know a lot of people in the US might not have heard of William and 1066 but he was a dynamic, charismatic figure, while the battle was a defining moment in history.'"

To do task 3

Get creative...

Design a news report on the Battle of Hastings – make sure that you include all the important facts and details, and make it captivating.

To do task 4

Source work

As described in Source A, a Hollywood film about Hastings is being planned. Design a storyboard as a basis for the film.

Hold tight boys!

Relatively safe in their well thought-out position, the English stood firm. The ferocious Housecarls were the first line of defence, swinging their massive battle axes at anybody who came near them. (These axes were quite capable of slicing a man and a horse in half.) Behind the Housecarls was the English shield wall, behind which stood the Fyrd and behind them was Harold (which was the safest place for him to be).

The Normans were lined up with the archers at the front, the foot soldiers behind the archers, the cavalry behind the foot soldiers and William behind them all.

In the English army, the shield wall protected the Housecarls if needed. Traditionally, archers could not operate effectively with a shield in one hand. It requires two hands to draw a bow, so holding a shield left them unable to fire arrows. This wasn't only a problem for the English though; it also presented a problem for William's troops: battles rely on both sides picking up arrows from the floor, perhaps even pulling them out of trees and fallen comrades, so that they can return fire at the opposition. The English sitting safely behind their shields meant that the Normans became short of arrows very quickly. The Norman arrows, which were fired high, up and over the shield wall rather than at it, were not being returned by the English, and they were largely ineffective because they were so far off-target. The English instead replied by hurling spears and using their sling-shots (hand-held catapults) from behind the shield wall.

Dead? I'm not dead!

The Norman battle plan was proving so ineffective, that a stroke of genius was required to break the **deadlock**. This came in unusual circumstances, when news spread that William was dead. So fierce had the fighting been that nobody had apparently noticed. This news caused the Breton troops (part of the Norman army) to panic and retreat. However it was soon revealed that it wasn't true, and the man to break this news to the troops was William himself.

A cunning plan – the Normans flee and the English follow.

Source B England the Autobiography,
John Lewis-Stempel, Penguin, 2006

"*Staying their retreat, he took off his helmet, and standing before them bare headed he cried 'Look at me well. I am still alive and by the grace of God I shall yet prove victor. What is the madness which makes you fly, and what way is open for your retreat? You are allowing yourselves to be pursued and killed by men whom you could slaughter like cattle. You are throwing away victory and lasting glory, rushing into ruin and incurring abiding disgrace. And all for naught since by flight none of you can escape destruction.'*"

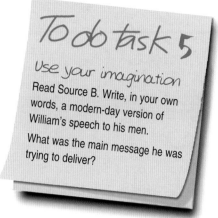

To do task 5
Use your imagination
Read Source B. Write, in your own words, a modern-day version of William's speech to his men.
What was the main message he was trying to deliver?

SPOTLIGHT

Shield walls were not just peculiar to the Norman Conquest; in fact they have been used throughout history to defend groups of soldiers. The Romans, in particular, used shields to protect their troops – a tactic often known as the 'Tortoise'.

Sensing an opportunity to finish the battle early, the English troops broke formation and ran after the Bretons who, unfortunately for the English, had just found out that William wasn't dead and that they really ought to continue fighting. They turned and hacked the English to the ground. Realising that this was a good way to break down the English defences, the 'strategy' was repeated. William's troops again turned and fled and many more English pursued them, only to be slaughtered when the Bretons turned on them once again. One of the fiercest warriors on the battlefield was William himself.

BUZZ WORDZZ

Rendezvous
Cavalry
Fyrd
Housescarl
Deadlock

The fighting went on well into the evening. By nightfall the battlefield was covered in blood, the dead and the dying, including Harold's two brothers – Gyrth and Leofwine. More importantly, Harold was dead. His body was so badly mangled and mutilated that he was only identified by birthmarks and blemishes on his body. Harold had been assassinated by a Norman 'hit squad' of four Knights who had hacked him to pieces or, as some people believe, shot him in the eye with an arrow.

This left William free to claim the title of King and he revelled in the name 'William the Conqueror'.

The Bayeux tapestry needs no introduction, but do you know:

- What it tells us?
- When and where it was produced?
  - Whether Harold was actually shot in the eye?

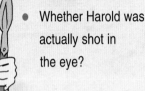

How long did it take you to make that?

One of the few sources of evidence about the Norman Conquest and the Battle of Hastings is the Bayeux tapestry. The Bayeux tapestry measures 230ft in length and is 20in high. It is a fantastic historical document, even though it is not on paper! The tapestry itself has long been the topic of debate and many people question whether today's tapestry is the original one. Its presence was not recorded in any historical document until 1476, before which it remained in relative obscurity. The name 'tapestry' is deceptive, however, as it is actually an embroidery on linen, rather than a woven tapestry. Legend states that it was commissioned by William the Conqueror's half-brother, Bishop Odo of Bayeux, to commemorate the Norman Conquest of England. Since its discovery it has been fascinating for historians to debate its origin and meaning and whether it is a true representation of the events of 1066.

Source A shows just how good the tapestry is at outlining the history behind William of Normandy's invasion of England.

To do task 1

Comprehension

1. How long is the Bayeux tapestry?
2. How is a tapestry made?
3. Who wanted to use the tapestry 850 years after it was first made?

Source A — The Bayeux Tapestry, *Carola Hicks*, Vintage Books, 2006

"The eye is carried along from left to right, not just by the excitement of the story, but by a whole series of sophisticated visual links; a character in one scene will point his finger towards the next, his body may be facing left, but his head and feet are already turning the other way. Trees and buildings serve as punctuation marks ending one incident and starting the next, yet the details enchant and delay. When you focus on any of the gesticulating groups of characters, a wealth of information about daily life emerges – clothes, tools and weapons, ornaments, digging a trench, planing a plank, how a horse clambers out of a ship, the trappings of falconry – all intricately depicted through dynamic little figures no more than a few centimetres high."

The Bayeux tapestry is open to interpretation but shows many events in detail.

However, some people believe that the tapestry has been altered over time, and therefore it may not be a reliable source of information. Various records of the tapestry have been made over time, three of which contain considerable differences.

Source B

Great Tales from English History, Robert Lacey, Little, Brown Book, 2007

"Two British historians, David Hill and John McSween, have recently compared the three versions and have discovered no less than 379 differences. Swords and stirrups appear and disappear. A griffin becomes an angel. A horse that was a mare in 1729 has by 1819 become a stallion. Freckles – or maybe acne – appear on a Norman shipbuilder's face as a result of some creative darning. Three shields become two, and fish turn into seals. Continuity seems to have gone by the board."

Is it just a piece of propaganda?

Some historians say that the tapestry is just a piece of propaganda and may not illustrate the true events of the beginning of the Norman Conquest. However this is debatable. Even if it wasn't meant to be a piece of propaganda, people have used it as such in recent history, for example the Nazis (see Source D).

So what does the tapestry actually tell us? For those of you who want to find out for yourselves, you could visit the original in Bayeux, Normandy, or the replica in the Museum of Reading. Perhaps you need to make up your own minds about whether it is fact or fiction.

Source C

Great Tales from English History, Robert Lacey, Little, Brown Book, 2007

"The most significant differences are in the successive depictions of Harold's slaying. In 1729 the King is grasping at the shaft of a spear that he could be trying to throw – or might, alternatively, be pulling out of his forehead. In 1819 the shaft has sprouted feathers, to become an arrow pointing towards his forehead. But fifty-three years later, in the photograph of 1872, the angle of the arrow has shifted downwards: now it is pointing directly into the King's right eye, which is hidden from us by the nose pieces of his helmet. This is what you see if you visit Bayeux today."

The First Crusade took place between AD 1095 and 1099.

Discussion POINT

Is the way that the Bayeux tapestry depicts events any worse than TV reporting today?

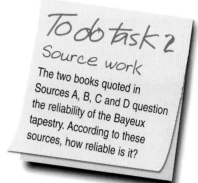

To do task 2

Source work

The two books quoted in Sources A, B, C and D question the reliability of the Bayeux tapestry. According to these sources, how reliable is it?

Source D

The Bayeux Tapestry, Carola Hicks, Vintage Books, 2006

"The significance of the Tapestry's message – a band of brave Germanic Knights defeating the dishonourable English and their arrogant leader – provided a marvellous propaganda opportunity for Joseph Goebbels and his team. To rub in the message, Goebbels' 'English voice', the Irishman William Joyce (Lord Haw Haw), made the Tapestry the subject of one of his broadcasts. In October 1941, he gloated on air that the tapestry would be toured and exhibited to the citizens of still neutral countries in order to warn of the imminent invasion of England."

A visit to any decent history museum reveals a wide collection of medieval weapons.

- What were they called?
  - What did they look like?
  - What were they used for?

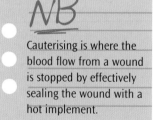

To do task 1

Comprehension

1. What are the main parts of a longbow?
2. What made a longbow a special weapon?
3. How many arrows could an archer fire in an hour?
4. What was a mantlet?
5. What is loading a crossbow called?

NB

Cauterising is where the blood flow from a wound is stopped by effectively sealing the wound with a hot implement.

BUZZ WORDZZ

Maiming
Mantlet
Mutilating
Quarrel

Spoiled for choice

Medieval weapons were particularly effective at **maiming** and **mutilating** people, severing limbs and ripping bodies open. Even if someone's arm or leg hadn't been taken off in one swift blow, it often had to be amputated, or at least cauterised in order to stop massive blood loss. Either way the victim was due a lot of pain. There was a huge variety of weapons available. So which to use?

The longbow

One weapon that nobody could afford to be without was the longbow (pictured below). If you had never seen a longbow before and were asked to describe it, what would you say? That's right – a bow, that's long – simple really.

A longbow wasn't quite so simple to make, however. The bowstave at the front had to be made from a certain type of wood – yew, hazel, ash or wych – and the string had to be made from carefully worked linen or hemp fibres. To be effective, all the materials had to be strong and resilient to withstand the constant firing of arrows. The arrows had to have their fletchings (feathers) made from goose feathers.

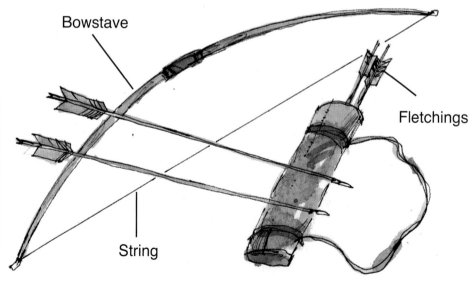

Bowstave

Fletchings

String

A longbow required between 75 and 100lbs of pressure to pull it back far enough to make it an effective weapon. Archers often had humped backs because of the tremendous amount of muscle they needed in the shoulders to draw the bowstring back. It was so hard to draw a bow back fully, that young men could not practise on full-sized longbows. They had to use 'short bows' that required less pressure.

Forced to practise

In the Middle Ages it was a legal requirement for all male English citizens at this time to be able to fire a bow and to practise firing one on a regular basis. Land owners often forced their subjects to use their bows regularly, so that they were ready in times of war.

Source A — The Bowmen of England, *Donald Featherstone, Jarrolds, 1967*

"King Edward I complained by letter to the Sheriff of London that archery had fallen into a grievous condition; he said that skill with the bow was put aside in favour of useless sports and he commanded that thereinafter the Sheriff should see to it that such idle practices were abandoned and that leisure time upon holidays should be spent in the noble pursuit of archery."

The effectiveness and importance of the longbow was not lost on Edward I.

This illustration from a medieval manuscript shows an army attacking a castle: longbowmen are at the front in the centre.

To do task 2
Get creative...
Design a poster persuading people that it is essential to practice using a longbow. Why was it so necessary?

So why use a bow?

The main benefit of the longbow was that it was accurate and could fire arrows quickly, at high velocity. When groups of archers fired their arrows at the same time, sending great hoards of them upon the advancing enemy, it was terrifying and deadly. To protect themselves from return fire, the archers had a shield called a '**mantlet**'. However it was difficult to use because both hands were needed to use the bow.

Besieging soldiers take cover as they shelter from rocks, debris and hot liquids thrown from the castle walls.

SPOTLIGHT

William de Braose was an important Norman Baron.

The source below shows just how powerful the bows were.

Source B — The Bowmen of England,
Donald Featherstone, Jarrolds, 1967

"A Knight of William de Braose was hit by an arrow which went through the skirt of his hauberk [chain mail coat], his mail hose, his thigh and through the leather and wood of his saddle and into his horse; when he swerved round another arrow pinned him in the same way by the other leg."

However some thought did have to go into the use of bows even though they had such killing power: archers had to carefully select the type of arrow that they would use under different circumstances (see Source C).

Source C — Bosworth 1485,
Christopher Gravett, Osprey Publishing, 2000

"A broadhead arrow was used against horses, with cutting edges to sever blood vessels and barbs to stop it falling out. More compact heads with small barbs seem to have been general purpose types. Needle-like bodkins could punch through mail, while against plate armour long bodkins could bore a hole sufficient to disable the man inside, provided they struck squarely and did not glance off."

A skilled archer could fire an arrow well over 380 yards and fire six arrows per minute. He would have access to 24 arrows in total that would be carried in a 'sheaf'. When he ran out of arrows he would pick up the arrows that had been fired at him and fire them back. The soil or blood that gathered on the arrowhead would add to the effectiveness of the weapon by spreading disease and infection within the wound.

Source D

Weapons that Made Britain,
from the Channel 4 Learning website

Anglo-Saxon shields would have been constructed using lindenwood (wood from the lime tree) and rawhide (cow skin). The Normans used kite shields – teardrop-shaped shields used on horseback – the shape of which gave protection against arrows on turning away from an attack. These shields are seen clearly on the Bayeux Tapestry.

Crossbows

Crossbows, different in design and build from the longbow, were used in battle but not commonly in England. They were used more on the continent. The main problem was that they were not as fast to load as a longbow and their range was not as great. They were very good, however, at sending their bolts through armour, up to a maximum range of about 300 yards.

Crossbows were a lot easier to use than longbows because they required less strength to fire them.

A close up of a crossbow and the metal-tipped bolt it fired.

The Normans had also targeted Italy in 1047, prior to attacking England.

Source E Castle,
Marc Morris, Channel 4 Books, 2003

*"The weapon was primed by pointing it nose to the ground, placing a foot on the stirrup and drawing back the bow with both hands – a practice known as 'spanning'. When the bowstring was fully drawn it engaged with a nut which held it in position. The weapon was then loaded by dropping a bolt or '**quarrel**' into the grooves on top, and perhaps securing it in place with a dab of beeswax."*

To do task 5

Get thinking...

Use the information on weapons included in this chapter to write an extended piece on Medieval weaponry. You must include the following paragraphs:
- types of weapons;
- effectiveness;
- the best weapon of all.

Crossbow men also used a shield called a 'pavise' to protect them when they were loading or 'spanning' the bow, as the loading of the weapon left them quite vulnerable.

The pavise was an effective shield.

Stop the Clock

Genghis Khan was born in 1162.

Axes and hand-held weapons

A hand-held weapon could be used instead of a bow. And there were plenty to choose from (see illustration below).

Bills, poleaxes (also called ravensbills), halberds, glaives, spears, pikes and battleaxes are just some of the weapons that could be used. All of these generally had long handles that allowed the weapon to be swung or stuck in the ground and pointed at charging foot soldiers or cavalry. The major difference between the weapons was the shape of the head that was fitted to the pole. Battleaxes could also be thrown if they had been fitted with short handles.

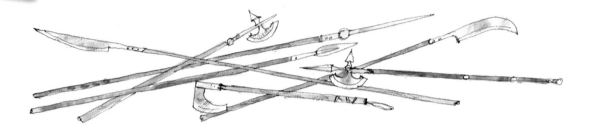

Maces

Maces were very effective weapons that had a round metal head on the end of a handle, with sharp protrusions added. They were heavy and often used to beat people around the head, and could dent armour so badly that the opponent had to be prised out of it.

All the weapons that were swung could apply massive amounts of power and pressure, and would have been terrifying to face.

Lances

These weapons were between 10 and 13ft long and were made from wood. During battle, the rounded tip that was used in tournaments was replaced with a sharp, pointed end that could be driven through the enemy. They are often thought of as the weapon of a Knight on horseback.

Swords

Numerous different types of swords could be used. Some had to be swung with one hand, while others had to be swung with both hands. Some had a single-edged blade while others had a double-edged blade. The type used was entirely down to personal preference.

Knights had to be proficient with a sword and they relied heavily upon it in battle.

To do task 6

Get creative...

You own a medieval weapons shop. Design a website homepage (on paper) that describes what you sell and why they would be effective.

Source F

Medieval Weapons,
from the About Britain website

"Living in a time when upheaval and warfare was commonplace, young medieval males were introduced to weaponry from quite an early age. Being able to handle a sword and wield it with subtlety, was the mark of a gentleman. Owning a sword was a great status-symbol, and these weapons were carefully looked after."

Other weapons

Anti-cavalry devices

One of the easiest ways to stop a horse in its tracks is to dig a pit on the battlefield, or a ditch around where you are positioned, and fill it with large wooden spikes. When the horses and riders galloped at you they would fall into the pit or ditch and be impaled on the spikes. Sometimes metal spikes called 'caltrops' (illustrated below) were employed and they did a huge amount of damage.

To do task 7
Source work
What does Source G tell us about the manufacture of gunpowder?

Guns and gunpowder

Guns were used widely during the Wars of the Roses (see pages 42–45), at the end of the Middle Ages. Many were cannon-like and had to be rolled or pulled onto battlefields. The musket also made an appearance during this period and armour was rendered useless by the sheer power that the musket generated.

Gunpowder (illustrated in a barrel, right), which is 10% carbon, 15% sulphur and 75% saltpetre (potassium nitrate), had to be manufactured in large quantities to enable the muskets and cannons to be fired. This had to be rammed down the barrel of the gun and then lit to propel the musket ball forwards. Loading the weapon was often slow and tedious, and could leave the user vulnerable to attack from the enemy.

Gunpowder was stored in barrels – by far the best way to keep it dry!

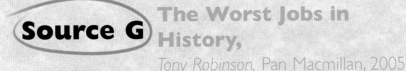

Source G | The Worst Jobs in History,
Tony Robinson, Pan Macmillan, 2005

"Gunpowder manufacture is an Arabic invention, described in a thirteenth-century book by Hassan Al-Rammah. Urine rich soil had to be mixed with ashes at a refinery. This mixture was then dissolved in water, boiled up in an evil smelling soup, and allowed to crystallize. The crystals were then mixed with glue or blood. The scum that rose to the top of the brew contained any remaining organic residue. Once this was removed, the mixture was re-crystallized and washed."

Discussion POINT?

How much of an impact has gunpowder had on warfare?

23

Knights in shining armour immediately bring a strong, bold image into the minds of most people. They are shrouded in mystery and a sense of heroism.

- What were the Knights really like?
- What did it take to become a Knight?

How did people become Knights?

Knights were normally chosen from among the ruling classes. It was very difficult, if not impossible, to become a Knight if you were a peasant. Knights were 'dubbed' and could then be called 'Sir'. The 'Knighting' ceremony that you might see occasionally on the news today is one that goes back to the Middle Ages, when the Lord of the Manor would rest his sword on the man's shoulders to symbolically demonstrate that he could behead him but wouldn't. Instead he chose to present him with a sword of his own, in the process making him a Knight. Once he had been made a Knight he had to fight for the Lord of the Manor, or else pay a tax in compensation. This tax was called 'scutage'.

Training

Knights weren't expected to arrive at their Knighting ceremony unprepared. They had to go through a considerable amount of training beforehand, over three distinct stages.

| Stage 1 – Page (7 – 14 years old) | Stage 2 – Squire (15 – 21 years old) | Stage 3 – Knight (over 21 years old) |

The training was based around the types of combat that a Knight would have to endure. Knights learned about swordsmanship, lance techniques, how to ride a horse properly and battle tactics. Only once they had mastered these skills would they be able to enter a tournament that would refine them even further.

Medieval tournaments

Although tournaments were intense, they were not usually deadly. Knights could practise jousting and the other skills that they had learned, within a relatively safe environment, although there was always the chance of death. More often, though, it was cracked bones and broken teeth that were the main injuries suffered. Tournaments were popular entertainment, with prize money to be won, so they always attracted large crowds.

To do task 1

Comprehension

1. How old did you have to be to become a squire?
2. What were solidi?
3. How much did armour cost?
4. What was an arming squire?

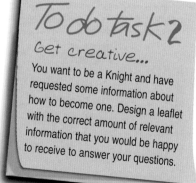

To do task 2

Get creative...

You want to be a Knight and have requested some information about how to become one. Design a leaflet with the correct amount of relevant information that you would be happy to receive to answer your questions.

Pay and conditions

Prize money and the spoils of war were an important part of a Knight's life because they were not paid for fighting – they were obliged to do so. This situation changed only when the Knight was recruited for additional service as a mercenary. This extra combat was paid for with coins known as 'solidi'. (Some people believe that this is where the word 'soldier' comes from.)

The Knight was compensated for poor pay by being able to keep anything that was captured during battle. The Lord of the Manor could also present the Knight with land for his good service. With this land came peasants for the Knight to rule over.

Knights, when acting as mercenaries, were often paid in 'solidi' – coins.

Armour

Knights could wear two different types of armour: chain-mail or plate armour. Both had their advantages and disadvantages. Chain-mail was light but didn't offer as much protection as plate armour, while plate armour was heavier and more bulky.

Every link and ring in the chain-mail armour had to be manufactured individually, which was time consuming and expensive. Plate armour was also very expensive to make, with the average price being around £50 – a huge amount of money at that time! The best armour came from the continent (specifically Germany and Flanders) and was very shiny. This shiny surface not only made the Knight look good, but it also meant that weapons would slide off the surface, spreading out the force of the blow.

A Knight's armour was made up from a number of different parts (as shown on the illustration to the right) that had to be put on in a specific order, including:

- sabatynes – steel shoes
- greaves – shin pieces
- vambraces – arm covers
- gauntlets – gloves.

NB

Flanders was the name of a territory that encompasses parts of modern France, Belgium and Holland.

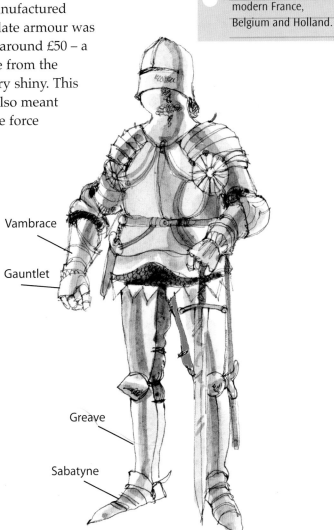

Vambrace

Gauntlet

Greave

Sabatyne

Knights at tournaments would practise jousting so that they were proficient at it in combat.

As all armour was very similar, Knights wore their coats of arms on their armour to enable people to recognise them. This was often who they were fighting for, rather than who they themselves were. These coats of arms would be on a jacket called a 'surcoat'.

Source A — Bosworth 1485,
Christopher Gravett,
Osprey Publishing, 2000

"Some Knights and Squires wore a tabard over their armour charged with their coat of arms. The tabard was a loose cloth covering put on over the head, with short, loose sleeves. Others might wear a long sleeved coat. Retainers might wear a livery jacket usually vertically divided into the two main colours of the Lord's arms, and with his badge."

To do task 3
Get creative...
A television company has asked you to prepare a programme on Knights. Design a storyboard to show what you would include.

Arming squires

A Knight was not able to function on his own. Imagine trying to mount a horse while carrying weapons and wearing a heavy suit of armour. A number of attendants were on hand to polish and clean the Knight's armour, and to help him get onto his horse. Looking after a Knight was done by an 'arming squire', which was a full-time and horrible job.

NB
Many Knights still wore chain-mail armour as well, as it was considerably lighter than solid armour.

Source B — The Worst Jobs in History,
Tony Robinson,
Pan Macmillan, 2005

"Throughout the day the Knight would get very messy indeed. Outside, he would be splattered with mud and the blood of horses and men, and as for the inside...most battles in the Middle Ages were fought in summer. Even when standing still, a Knight would have sweated buckets. Imagine how much would have poured off him during the height of battle. And that was just the top half. The bottom half would have been even worse, particularly if the Knight had been very afraid. It would have been hell in there."

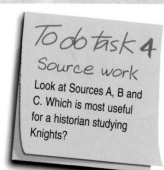

To do task 4
Source work
Look at Sources A, B and C. Which is most useful for a historian studying Knights?

Fighting in armour was thirsty work and would guarantee good weight loss. A large intake of water was required, so the arming squire was also responsible for supplying that. However, by the fifteenth century the weight of a full suit of armour had been reduced to about 50lb, which made it a lot easier to wear, ride and fight in; also making the job of the arming squire easier.

War horses

Knights relied heavily on their war horses. These were especially chosen for their bravery and strength. They had to carry the full weight of the Knight, his armour and his weapons.

The war horse itself had to wear armour:

- neck – crinet
- head – chanfron
- front – peytral
- sides – flanchard
- rear – crupper.

Killing

The role of a Knight was to avoid being killed and, in the process, to kill as many people as possible, as quickly as possible. The code of 'chivalry' among Knights suggested that it wasn't exactly proper to kill people from the 'upper classes' of society, so this was generally avoided, although it was impossible to avoid doing so in the heat of battle.

Stop the Clock
The massive stone heads on Easter Island can be dated back to approximately 1300 CE.

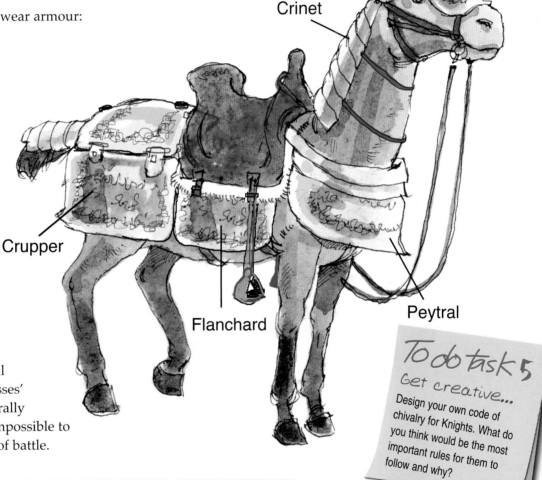

Chanfron

Crinet

Crupper

Flanchard

Peytral

To do task 5
Get creative...
Design your own code of chivalry for Knights. What do you think would be the most important rules for them to follow and why?

Source C Medieval Lives, Terry Jones, BBC Books, 2004

"The ability to beat another man to a pulp or cut him into bloody pieces was not only a requirement of Knighthood – it was one of its ideals. Richard the Lionheart, for example, was celebrated amongst the Knightly class for his ability to chop his victim's skulls down to the teeth."

Discussion POINT

How much alike are medieval Knights and modern soldiers?

27

Castles were the ultimate in secure housing, but they were also the ultimate in uncomfortable living.

- Why were they built with such a need for safety?
- How difficult was it to get into them?

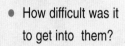

Castles, castles everywhere

You don't have to travel far to find a castle; when you travel across England and Wales, you can't miss them. The past is stamped boldly on the landscape for all to see. Most of the castles in England, Scotland and Wales were built between 1066 and 1284, during the Norman Conquest, and later to control the Welsh. These castles were the centre of many local communities and were for living in, not just for defensive measures.

Stone castles were very expensive to build, but when money was no object they were by far the best choice. They were strong and therefore easy to defend: stone is, of course, more resilient and fireproof than wood.

However, the first castles that appeared were made from wood and were called motte and **bailey** castles. The 'bailey' was a central area that was surrounded by a wooden fence or '**palisade**'. Inside the bailey was the 'motte': a mound that the keep (main tower) was placed on. The bailey also contained numerous residential buildings, cattle, sheep and supplies.

Living in a castle

Striking a balance between comfort for those who lived in a castle and the defensive necessities of those defending them was difficult. In most cases the defence had to come first. This meant that castles were not very comfortable places to live. Electricity was a long way from being discovered and lighting was provided by torches made from lit reeds and large fires. This meant that castles were very dark. Heat was also provided by torches and fires, and heat loss was prevented by hanging tapestries on the walls, and spreading reeds and rushes on the floor, together with some rugs. Narrow corridors and stone floors made the castles even darker, colder and more depressing. Many people therefore chose not to live in castles, except in times of absolute necessity.

Large supplies of food and water were stockpiled within the castle to ensure that, if the castle was placed under siege, the inhabitants could hold out for a very long time. This food had to be salted or spiced to ensure that it did not turn bad.

Source A

Life in a Medieval Castle,

Brenda Ralph Lewis, The History Press, 2007

"In Lancaster castle in 1215, for instance, 80 cows and 130 sheep were quartered in the Bailey. Ample stocks of bacon, ham, herring and other fish were salted and preserved. Stores of barrels were filled to the brim with grains and beans. Supplies of wine and malt and barley were also stockpiled. Corn was brought into the castle in bulk, to be ground by hand when required. Cheese, bread, rice, figs, raisins and even eels were stored in quantity."

To do task 1
Comprehension

1. What is a 'bailey'?
2. How was heat provided in a castle?
3. Where were castles commonly situated?

Where to position a castle

Before a castle was built, a suitable site had to be chosen. The best place was on high ground. This gave the defenders the advantage of being able to look down upon any attackers. Some castles were built on high rock outcrops. Edinburgh Castle and Stirling Castle are two good examples.

Other factors also had to be taken into consideration when building a castle, such as the methods used by attackers during a siege. For example, building a castle on a rock base would deter enemy attempts at mining under the foundations. Proximity to fresh water and **strategic** location, such as being close to a river, were other factors to consider.

To do task 2
Use your imagination...
What would be the perfect castle location? List your top ten requirements, giving reasons for your choices.

▼ Edinburgh Castle is built on a volcanic outcrop.

To do task 3
Get creative...
Design a brief job advert for a Castellan. What does the job involve? Who would be most suitable for the job and why?

Defending a castle

Many castles had numerous defensive barriers to deter and delay attackers. Beaumaris Castle on Anglesey, North Wales, was designed with 14 defensive barriers, including a moat, drawbridge, portcullises, murder slots, vast doors, spy holes and internal walls. It would have been like a massive obstacle course for an enemy trying to make its way into the centre of the castle.

Beaumaris Castle is on the island of Anglesey, North Wales, and was designed to be defended easily.

Source B

Life in a Medieval Castle,
*Brenda Ralph Lewis,
The History Press, 2007*

"He was responsible for every detail of the castle defences from the state of the garrison's weaponry and ammunition to the soundness of the castle's structure, the security of the castle, even the depth of the water in the moat."

The role of a Castellan

The man in overall charge of maintaining the castle defences was called the **Castellan**. Castles were designed to be defended by the minimum of people and therefore the defences had to be ingenious and easily manned (see Source B).

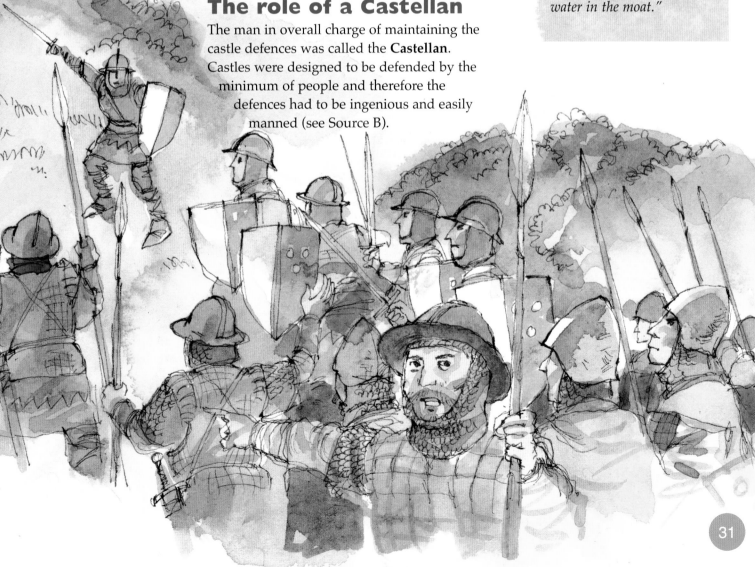

Castle walls often contained towers for added defence.

The castle walls

Before the cannon was invented, one of the main ways to keep people from entering a castle was to build very thick walls. Sometimes these were more than 20ft thick. When Rochester Castle was placed under siege in 1215, the attackers had a real challenge ahead of them as it had walls that were about 13ft thick and 125ft high.

Some castle builders even went so far as to build multiple sets of walls – these were called concentric castles.

An example is Caerphilly Castle, which was built with a double wall which made the castle very easy to defend. The outer wall was lower than the inner, so that both walls could be defended at the same time without any loss of vision in any direction.

Castle builders could also attach wooden extensions to the castle walls, which jutted out and allowed the defenders to drop objects onto the people who were attacking. These were known as 'hoardings'.

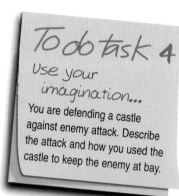

To do task 4

Use your imagination...

You are defending a castle against enemy attack. Describe the attack and how you used the castle to keep the enemy at bay.

Towers

Castles were usually built with towers, which were often round in shape. A round tower gave the defenders several advantages – the enemy were always visible and could not dig under any corners, which would weaken the tower's structure. Some towers were square however. Tower roofs were usually pointed and sloping so that missiles hurled at them would bounce or slide off.

Moats

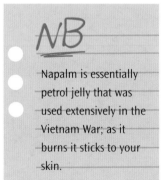

NB

Napalm is essentially petrol jelly that was used extensively in the Vietnam War; as it burns it sticks to your skin.

Many castles were built by the sea or open stretches of water, to allow easy access for supplies. Moats were built for defence. They were too deep to wade across and stopped attackers getting very close to the walls of the castle. To allow the occupiers of the castle to get in and out without using a boat, a drawbridge was installed. This could be raised or lowered depending upon whether the castle was under siege.

Defenders could also stop people trying to cross the moat by using Greek fire – a substance that has been described as an ancient version of Napalm. Essentially it set the water of the moat on fire. Greek fire is made from oil and quicklime, and is almost impossible to put out with water.

The keep

The keep is the strongest, most easily defended part of the castle. Keeps were also called 'donjons'.

The keep was the last place of safety for the inhabitants of the castle. It was designed purely for survival. There was just one door to get in and out. The keep was always made of stone, with the only wooden part being the floor. Some keeps were surrounded by an additional moat and wall as two final defensive barriers. If the walls were breached, the defenders could withdraw into the keep, shut the door and barricade it with furniture and anything else that came to hand.

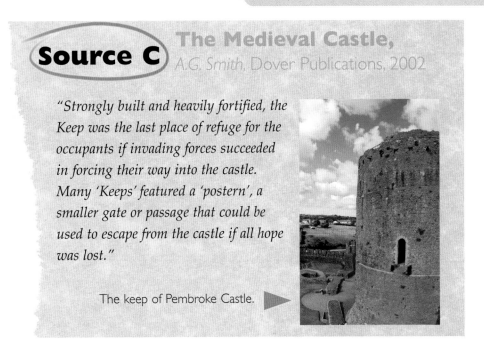

Source C — The Medieval Castle, A.G. Smith, Dover Publications, 2002

"Strongly built and heavily fortified, the Keep was the last place of refuge for the occupants if invading forces succeeded in forcing their way into the castle. Many 'Keeps' featured a 'postern', a smaller gate or passage that could be used to escape from the castle if all hope was lost."

The keep of Pembroke Castle.

Barbicans

Castle builders sometimes added a fortified gatehouse called a barbican. This usually contained a **portcullis** (see below) and various devices that would deter attackers.

To do task 5

Get creative...

You are attacking a castle. Formulate your plan of attack and draw a diagram using the equipment detailed on these pages.

Portcullis

Most people know that a portcullis is a large, strongly built gate that slammed down to keep attackers out of the castle. It was sometimes backed up by a second gate that would trap attackers within the barbican or gatehouse so that the defenders could throw missiles and other deadly objects at them.

Go on, throw something at him!

Various openings in castle walls or in the ceilings of gatehouses allowed defenders to throw objects at their attackers below. These holes were known as 'machicolations', 'brattishes' and 'murder holes'. Stories are told of hot oil being thrown on the attackers, but sheer expense may have made this impossible. Hot water was far cheaper.

Arrow loops

Archers could fire volleys of arrows through narrow slits in the castle walls with little risk of being hit by fire from the attackers. These were eventually modified into gun loops, so that muskets could be used instead of bows.

A barbican – a fortified gatehouse.

Far better to be coming down a staircase than going up it.

A siege tower.

A trebuchet.

A mangonel. ▶

Spiral staircases

You might not think that a staircase was a defensive feature but Medieval swordsmen usually swung their swords with their right hands, so if the staircase spiralled clockwise it would only allow those who were coming downstairs to swing their swords.

Attacking a castle

The defenders of the castles were cunning, but so were the attackers. The attackers had various methods of storming castles, including those featured below.

Siege towers

These were towers on wheels that could be pushed up to the wall of the castle (provided it didn't have a moat). They would be built to the same height as the castle walls and the attackers would climb ladders inside the tower to reach the top. Often hides or skins would be stretched across the tower to provide protection from arrows or missiles while the attackers climbed upwards. Once at the top, a small drawbridge would be lowered onto the top of the walls and the attackers could run straight from the tower onto the walls. Siege towers were most effective when used on flat, firm surfaces, as they were heavy and hard to handle.

Scaling ladders

Attackers could also lean long ladders up against the castle walls – these were known as scaling ladders. However, they were ineffective against extremely high walls and were easily pushed away from the walls by defenders. It needed a very brave man to climb one.

Catapults

Large catapults, called trebuchets and mangonels, could be used to launch large missiles at castle walls. The trebuchet could fire large rocks or boulders over a considerable distance. It was basically a machine that had a very long throwing arm. This long arm was counterbalanced by a large weight, which, when released, propelled the arm forwards and upwards, hurling whatever had been placed in it (often balls of flaming pitch or large rocks) at the castle or over the walls. Some of these trebuchets were 50ft long and the missiles fired from trebuchets could be as heavy as 310lb.

Mangonels originated in Rome. They were not as efficient as the trebuchets and could only fire relatively small missiles over a moderate range.

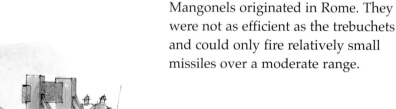

Battering rams

Another way to breach the castle walls was with a battering ram: a tree trunk re-enforced with metal at the end. This was repeatedly bashed against the castle door or walls. Sometimes a drill was used to weaken the castle walls before the battering ram was used. This drill removed mortar from between the stones in the walls.

Mining

Miners, or 'sappers', sometimes tried to dig underneath the castle walls, either to gain access or to weaken the walls. To combat this form of attack, people built castle walls with bases that extended outwards, so that defenders could easily spot anyone trying to mine underneath.

Attackers of wooden castles often filled holes under the walls with wood and other flammable materials. Burning the materials would weaken the foundations and then set fire to the castles themselves. However, this was little use against stone castles. Tales of the siege of Rochester Castle suggest that pig fat may have been used to make the fires burn faster and more furiously (see Source D).

Occasionally, defenders might dig towards the attackers – called counter-mining – to try and thwart their efforts.

Filling in the moat

Attempts were often made by attackers to fill in the moats, using pieces of old timber and stones, to allow battering rams and siege towers to be pushed over the moat and up to the castle walls.

Cannons

The introduction of huge cannons called bombards meant that castles could be targeted effectively whatever the defensive arrangements were, and from a considerable distance. They were introduced during the fifteenth century.

Whatever method was used, until the introduction of cannons, getting into any castle was a very difficult task.

A bombard.

Source D

Castle,
Marc Morris,
Channel 4 Books, 2003

"Once the mine was finished it would have been stuffed with brushwood, straw and kindling to feed a great fire. How the pig fat was introduced is a matter of debate. An older generation of more imaginative historians envisaged the forty strong herd being driven into the tunnels while still alive, burning torches tied to their tails. Sadly, modern military experts now think this unlikely."

BUZZ WORDZZ

Bailey
Castellan
Palisade
Portcullis
Strategic

To do task 6

Get thinking...

You have been asked to rate the methods of attacking castles out of ten. Place them in order of perceived effectiveness and give them all a score.

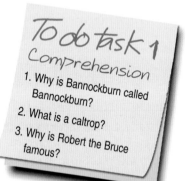

Bannockburn and the events that led to a famous victory for the Scots, marked a major turning point for the people of Scotland.

● How did Robert the Bruce engineer such an important victory?

The location of the site of the Battle of Bannockburn.

Why is this battle so important?

The Battle of Bannockburn took place on 24 June 1314. It is one of the most famous battles in English history and was the most important event in the Scottish Wars of Independence. These wars took place between 1295 and 1318, as the Scots sought freedom and independence from the rule of England.

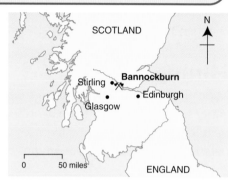

Bannockburn is located near Stirling, in Scotland. It is on this site that King Edward II suffered a humiliating defeat against the Scottish army led by Robert the Bruce. (Edward's father, Edward I's nickname was 'the hammer of the Scots' but his son didn't live up to it on this occasion.)

To do task 1

Comprehension

1. Why is Bannockburn called Bannockburn?
2. What is a caltrop?
3. Why is Robert the Bruce famous?

Source A

The Bowmen of England,
Donald Featherstone, Jarrolds, 1967

"The encounter was most unequal but Bruce did not decline it, and rode forward to meet him in full career. Just as they were about to close he swerved his hackney round, and as de Bohun's lance passed harmlessly, he clove his head and helmet in twain with one blow of his battle axe and laid him dead at his feet. The weapon was shivered by the violence of the stroke, and to those who blamed him for his temerity, Bruce replied simply: 'I have broken my good battle axe.'"

Who was Robert the Bruce?

Robert the Bruce (pictured left) was born into an aristocratic family on 11 July 1274. He was a dignified, proud man who was an effective warrior. Famed for his bravery and courage, he was the perfect man to lead the Scots towards their freedom. Just before the main battle began, he showed why he was such a feared warrior when he met Sir Henry de Bohun, who was attempting to capture him (see Source A).

He was so certain of his own ability that Bruce had even discarded his helmet in favour of a crown, which he wore onto the battlefield.

The two sides face each other

Two very different armies lined up, eager to begin the battle. The English had large numbers of cavalry and the Scottish had lots of infantry. This essentially pitted the charging, chivalrous Knights of England against the slow-moving pike men of Scotland. The Scots used effective formations called 'schiltroms' which relied on the pike men forming tight circles with their weapons facing outwards. These could be employed as a stationary or mobile defencive force.

Edward II needed this victory so much that he provided all his Knights with armour and weapons – all they had to provide was their own horse. The stage was set, but who would be the victors?

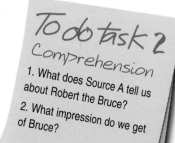

To do task 2

Comprehension

1. What does Source A tell us about Robert the Bruce?
2. What impression do we get of Bruce?

The tactics

Bruce had cunningly chosen to position his army in a difficult area of hilly ground close to the River Forth, at a place called New Park. Here he lined up his troops near a small burn (stream) called Bannock.

Outnumbered, the only real defence that the Scottish had against the English cavalry was a huge pit that they had dug and filled with stakes, condemning any men on horseback to a plunge to their death. They also had rows of metal spikes, called 'caltrops', which stuck up out of the ground, designed to slash open the legs of horses. In the front line of their defences were rows of pikes, positioned to challenge the onslaught of the English (as shown in the above illustration).

When the charge came, the English cavalry was unable to penetrate the wall of pikes. Those who weren't killed outright began to retreat. The Scots launched an attack on the English archers, and confusion soon broke out among the English forces. The Scottish pike men then advanced towards them, forcing them back towards a small gorge. The Scottish had one more trick to ensure complete breakdown of the English organisation: a fake counter-attack (see Source C).

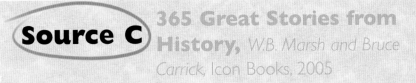

Source C 365 Great Stories from History, W.B. Marsh and Bruce Carrick, Icon Books, 2005

"The brutal slogging match might have ended as a bloody draw but for an ingenious ruse that decided the day. A force of Scottish camp followers – grooms, priests, cooks and porters – emerged from the forest on the English left, waving banners and shouting in simulation of a counter-attack. The English, hesitating at what appeared to be a fresh army sent against them, began to withdraw, slowly at first, but soon in panic."

Against all odds, the Scots won. Many British soldiers had fallen into Bannockburn, where they met their maker, earning themselves a place in history.

Source B

Bannockburn, from the Undiscovered Scotland website

On the southern edge of Stirling is the Bannockburn Heritage Centre, run by the National Trust for Scotland. Here, and in the neighbouring parkland, Scotland commemorates, and to a degree celebrates, what most people view as the most significant victory won by Scotland over an invading English army.

The general background to the Battle of Bannockburn is clearly established. Robert the Bruce, or Robert I, crowned himself King of Scotland in March 1306. He then spent a number of years seeking to consolidate his hold on power in the face of the largely ineffectual efforts of Edward II of England and, initially at least, the much more dangerous opposition of his Scottish enemies.

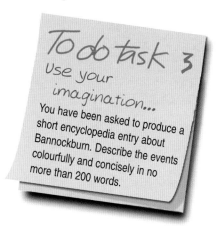

To do task 3

Use your imagination...

You have been asked to produce a short encyclopedia entry about Bannockburn. Describe the events colourfully and concisely in no more than 200 words.

Discussion POINT

Should Scotland still be a separate country from England?

Agincourt may not be top of your list of battles, but it was an important victory for the English, even if it was not actually meant to happen.

- Why did the French and English clash at Agincourt?
- Why were the French so badly beaten?

Why was there a battle at Agincourt?

Since the Norman invasion in 1066, the relationship between France and England had been a difficult one. Situated only 22 miles from each other at the closest point, control over France was always a temptation for the English. Between the mid-fourteenth and mid-fifteenth centuries, a series of battles were fought between France and England, largely over disputed territory and trade. This period became known as the Hundred Years War. By 1415, the temptation of taking the French throne proved too much for King Henry V of England, so he and his invasion force made their way across the channel.

Source A — England the Autobiography, John Lewis Stempel, Viking, 2005

"On 11th August 1415 at the head of 10,000 soldiers, Henry V sailed to France, claiming its throne as his. After besieging and capturing Harfleur (which took from 19 August to 22 September), Henry tramped across the Normandy countryside towards Calais with the intention of tempting the French into battle. At Agincourt, a French army of some 30,000 decided to oblige. Siege, disease and garrisoning duties had reduced the English force to around 5,000."

To do task 1
Comprehension
1. Where is Agincourt?
2. Which English king fought at Agincourt?
3. When did the Battle of Agincourt take place?
4. What illness did the English archers suffer from?

The Battle of Agincourt took place on 25 October 1415. Situated close to Calais, Agincourt was never meant to be the scene of a great battle. It happened there more by chance than through good planning. After Harfleur (see Source A), time to continue the conquest of France was not on the side of Henry V, as the traditional campaigning season was coming to an end.

Many of you have heard of Calais, but how many have heard of Agincourt? This map shows the location of the Battle of Agincourt, close to the River Somme.

NB
If you go on a school trip to the battlefields of World War I, you will be extremely close to the site of Agincourt as well.

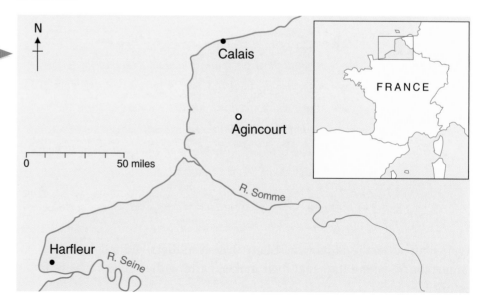

Henry had to make the decision whether to continue or return to England.

The decision was made to return to England and as Henry's troops marched along the River Somme, trying to find a suitable crossing point, they met the French. The French followed the English along the river bank and, when the English finally managed to cross the river, the French managed to cut off their route to Calais and home. Realising that there was no other option but to take on the French army, the troops clashed at Agincourt.

To do task 2
Research
Agincourt is not the only battle to take place near the River Somme. Find out about another famous battle at this location.

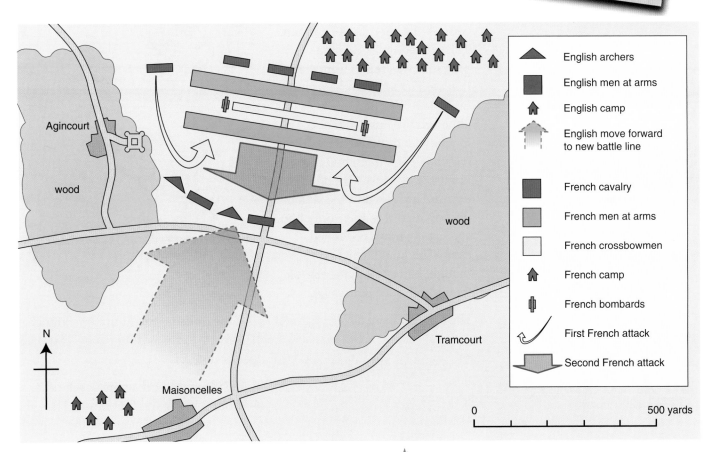

The line-up of the troops at Agincourt.

Source B — **Great Tales from English History,**
Robert Lacey,
Little, Brown Book, 2000

"Henry V was addressing his small, damp and beleaguered army outside the village of Agincourt in northern France. Here the English had been disconcerted to find their route back to Calais blocked by an immensely larger French army. Modern estimates put the English at 6,000, facing as many as 20,000 or even 25,000. Henry's cause looked hopeless."

Source C

The Agincourt Carol,
From the Channel 4 History website

"Owre kynge went forth to Normandy, With grace and myyt of chivalry; The God for hym wrouyt marvelously, Wherefore Englonde may calle, and cry Deo gratias: Deo gratias redde pro victoria."

The fighting

The English army was hugely outnumbered and facing a humiliating defeat. Victory would only come with great bravery and a good dose of cunning. Both sides had cavalry at their disposal and could employ a weapon that had been specifically designed to counter the charging horsemen. This weapon was called a paling. It was made from stakes that were stuck into the ground. Both sides also had bows, although the English had the longbow and the French had the crossbow. The main body of the English army was actually made up from archers and the skill of the bowmen was their only hope against the massive French army. The English archers, though, had something else on their minds (see Source D).

Source D

History Without the Boring Bits,
Ian Crofton,
Quercus Publishing, 2007

"At the battle of Agincourt many of the English archers – who played such a key role in devastating the flower of French chivalry – were suffering from dysentery. Unable to leave their posts to relieve themselves, they fought naked from the waist down, and allowed nature to take its course."

The English were also concerned about the unusual threat that the French had made to them if they were captured (see Source E).

Both sides faced off against each other without making the first move. Then the French horsemen charged at the English, but through a narrow, wooded route. This condensed the target for the British archers, who could concentrate their fire-power on a much narrower band of soldiers.

As the French charged they soon realised that they were in trouble. While the English bowmen rained their arrows down upon the French, the French Knights in armour trudged through the woods towards their position. Bogged down in mud after heavy rain and struggling to get any grip with their feet, the French were becoming even more vulnerable to the English archers (see Source F).

Source E

An Utterly Impartial History of Britain,
John O'Farrell, Black Swan, 2008

"The Bow was drawn with two fingers, which the French had promised they would cut off every English prisoner they captured. And so, as an act of defiance, the English peasant soldier stuck these two fingers up at the French, which remains a peculiarly British rude gesture to this day."

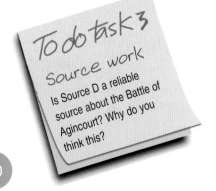

To do task 3
Source work
Is Source D a reliable source about the Battle of Agincourt? Why do you think this?

The final figures

The Battle of Agincourt was a total disaster for the French. Estimates suggest that the French lost between 7,000–10,000 men, while the English only lost 100 soldiers in total.

To do task 4
Get creative...

You have been asked to design a page on Agincourt for a children's history book. Set out the page on A4 plain paper and write a simple description suitable for primary school children. Think about how much information you would need to include for young children below 11 years of age.

Source F — **The Worst Jobs in History,** *Tony Robinson, Pan Macmillan, 2005*

"The rains that had plagued the English now worked to their advantage. It made the ground in front of their position a quagmire, which trapped the French cavalry under a hail of English arrows. The French Knights were protected by plate armour, but their horses weren't. Wounded steeds threw their riders into the mud, then careered through the close-packed ranks of French foot soldiers as they tried to shake off the hail of English arrows.

"They became such an easy target for the bowmen that thousands fell amongst the showers of arrows. When the English bowmen ran out of arrows they took up their other weapons and waded into the French, standing on top of the corpses to get a more effective position."

Stop the Clock

People have been attending Oxford University since 1096.

The Wars of the Roses mark a major turning point in British history, bringing the Tudors to the throne of England.

- How did the struggle for the throne of England become so complicated?
- Why did this result in a war that lasted over 30 years?

The white rose was the symbol of the House of York and the red rose was the symbol of the House of Lancaster.

To do task 1

Comprehension

1. Why are they called the 'Wars of the Roses'?
2. When did the Wars of the Roses end?
3. According to the map on page 42, how many battles made up the Wars of the Roses?

The Wars of the Roses left little of England and Wales untouched.

Stop the clock

July 1290 saw Edward I expelling all Jews from England.

Why were they fought?

The 'Wars of the Roses' is the name given to a series of battles for the English throne, fought between two families: the House of Lancaster and the House of York. The wars began in May 1455 and did not end until 1487. Over the years, key players changed but the wars continued. The wars had all but ended by the time that Henry Tudor was crowned King in 1485, although there was one further battle at Stoke when the new King's position was challenged one last time.

Why are they called the 'Wars of the Roses'?

The name 'Wars of the Roses' comes from the emblems of the two families involved. The House of Lancaster had a red rose as its symbol and the House of York had a white rose. (Modern cricket matches between Lancashire and Yorkshire are now called 'Roses' matches'; the Lancashire team has a red rose on its shirts and the Yorkshire team has a white rose.) The name 'Wars of the Roses' has been given to that period in relatively recent history and was not used at the time.

The claimants to the throne of England

Both the House of York and the House of Lancaster had a claim to the throne through Edward III, as shown in the family tree opposite. Both families came from a family line known as the 'Plantagenets'. The family tree shown is abbreviated for simplicity. Research the family tree in more detail and add some more complex details to clarify the family links.

The major battles

The Wars of the Roses were made up from a large number of individual battles, which took place over a long period of time.

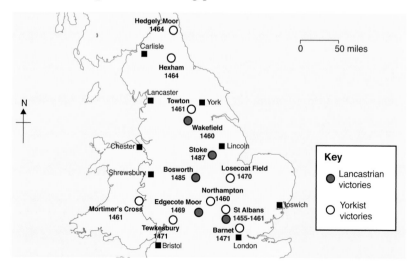

Although the Battle of Bosworth is seen by many as the end of the Wars of the Roses, they actually concluded at the Battle of Stoke on 16 June 1487.

The soldiers

The Wars of the Roses saw a large mix of soldiers, ranging from professionals who had seen action during the Hundred Years War to soldiers who had been recruited especially for these wars. The army of England at this time was largely cobbled together from part-time soldiers and volunteers. They had relatively little training and could be aged from 16 to 60.

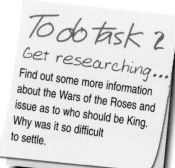

To do task 2
Get researching...
Find out some more information about the Wars of the Roses and issue as to who should be King. Why was it so difficult to settle.

Source A Bosworth 1485,
Christopher Gravett, Osprey Publishing, 2000

"Towns and cities were expected to pay for the muster of urban militias, summoned usually by royal letters. Mercenaries also appeared in the English armies, as well as troops sent by supportive foreign allies. Men who were not retainers fought for wages, ... enhanced by the prospect of loot on the battlefield. Thus any equipment received from their Lord might be improved after actual combat. The result would be a very varied appearance in troop bodies, the only uniformity being in the livery colours or badges worn by a Lord's men."

To do task 3
Get researching...
1. Who were the Princes in the Tower?
2. Why did their disappearance allow Richard III to become King?

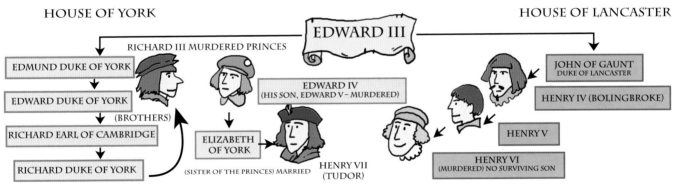

Source B

Source B The Princes in the Tower,
Alison Weir, Pimlico, 1992

"There are few people who have not heard of the Princes in the Tower, just as there are few people who do not relish a good murder or mystery story. In the cases of the Princes, we have an especially fascinating mystery, not only because they were royal victims who lived in a particularly colourful age, nor because there are plenty of clues as to their fate, but because speculation as to what happened to them has provoked controversy for many hundreds of years. Even today, the battle still rages between those who believe that the Princes were murdered by their Uncle, Richard III, and the revisionists, who have forwarded several attractive theories to the contrary."

Although the Wars of the Roses officially concluded at the Battle of Stoke in 1487, Bosworth is seen as the major watershed.

- How did Henry Tudor eventually get his hands on the throne of England?
- What happened to Richard?

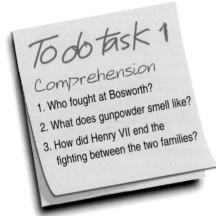

Henry's here

Henry Tudor landed at Milford Haven, South Wales, in 1485 with the sole aim of finding Richard III and taking the throne from him.

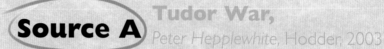

Source A — Tudor War, Peter Hepplewhite, Hodder, 2003

"He [Henry Tudor] was a young rebel, eager to seize the throne. He marched north through Wales and called on his supporters to join him. The King, Richard III, summoned his armies and caught Henry at Bosworth Field in Leicestershire. Two hours of bitter fighting later, Richard was dead. England had a new King, Henry VII."

Henry Tudor based his forces at White Moors, while Richard's army took up position at the top of Ambion Hill. Richard's army had the advantage of controlling the higher ground and he also had more men. Henry Tudor's army may have been as large as 8,000, but Richard had around 16,000 troops at his disposal.

The fighting

The smell of rotten eggs (the odour of gunpowder) wafted across the battlefield as Richard's army unleashed its guns on the Lancastrians. These guns were mostly cannons called 'bombards' and 'serpentines'. The men were armed with muskets.

To do task 1

Comprehension

1. Who fought at Bosworth?
2. What does gunpowder smell like?
3. How did Henry VII end the fighting between the two families?

Muskets were deadly at close range: the first truly effective firearm.

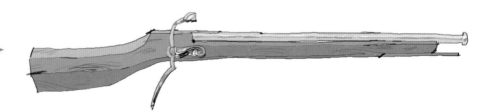

To do task 2

Source work

Read sources A, B and C. What do they tell you about Henry Tudor, Richard III and the Battle of Bosworth? Do you think that they are useful to somebody studying the Wars of the Roses and are they reliable sources of information?

Henry's army simply marched out of range of the cannons, ready to begin the battle on foot, so the archers on both sides let loose their arrows. The foot soldiers stood ready, armed with long pikes and bills. Then Richard's men charged down Ambion Hill and the two armies clashed hand to hand. Richard charged with them (see Source B).

However, Richard's confidence resulted in his death.

Source B

Bosworth 1485,
Christopher Gravett, Osprey Publishing, 2000

"Richard thundered down the south-west slopes on to the plain below, heading straight for Henry Tudor. His royal standard bearer with him, his courageous charge – 'the swan song of Medieval English chivalry' as it has been called – must have been exhilarating, and meant action at last for the soldier King. He may well have roared his motto 'Loyaulte me lie!' to rally both himself and his followers."

The end of the wars

Ambion Hill as it is today.

Source C

The History of Britain and Ireland,
Kenneth Morgan, Mike Corbishley, J. Gillingham, Rosemary Kelly, Ian Dawson and James Mason,
Oxford University Press, 1996

"He bore himself like a noble soldier and honourably defended himself to his last breath, shouting again and again that he was betrayed, and crying 'Treason!, Treason! Treason!' "

The first printed book was published in 1477.

Discussion POINT?

Should anybody be allowed to be king or queen?

The defeat of Richard of York meant that Henry Tudor finally had his hands on the throne of England. To guarantee future stability, he united the House of Lancaster and the House of York by marrying Elizabeth of York. Their red and white roses were amalgamated in the Tudor rose (pictured right). However, as mentioned before, Bosworth was not the last battle – the last battle was the Battle of Stoke, where a man called Lambert Simnel (claiming to be the nephew of Edward IV) was also defeated in battle by Henry.

Why does this rose symbolise the union of the two warring families?

Chapter 2
War during Tudor and Stuart times

Introduction

The Tudor and Stuart periods were times of uprisings and upheaval. Disagreements over religious beliefs and an increasing desire for individual rights and freedoms prompted conflict, aggression and warfare. This time was not just about the fate of individual monarchs, it was a period in which violent warfare evolved.

Who ruled?

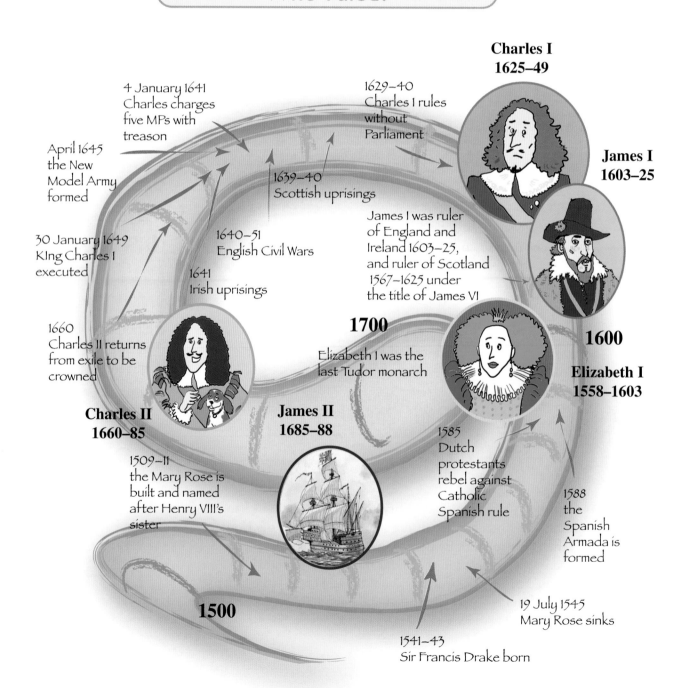

Charles I
1625–49

4 January 1641
Charles charges
five MPs with
treason

1629–40
Charles I rules
without
Parliament

April 1645
the New
Model Army
formed

1639–40
Scottish uprisings

James I
1603–25

James I was ruler
of England and
Ireland 1603–25,
and ruler of Scotland
1567–1625 under
the title of James VI

30 January 1649
King Charles I
executed

1640–51
English Civil Wars

1641
Irish uprisings

1700

Elizabeth I was the
last Tudor monarch

1600

1660
Charles II returns
from exile to be
crowned

Charles II
1660–85

James II
1685–88

Elizabeth I
1558–1603

1585
Dutch
protestants
rebel against
Catholic
Spanish rule

1509–11
the Mary Rose is
built and named
after Henry VIII's
sister

1588
the
Spanish
Armada is
formed

1500

19 July 1545
Mary Rose sinks

1541–43
Sir Francis Drake born

Why was the navy so important?

All the battles mentioned in Chapter 1 were fought on land, but in Tudor times the real strength of Britain lay in the navy. As an island, Britain was a difficult place to conquer but a strong navy was essential if the kingdom was to remain safe and secure. Henry VII and Henry VIII invested large amounts of money to build more ships, both for fighting and trading. By the reign of Henry VIII, England's navy was a **formidable** force with some magnificent ships. Records show that ships such as *Pauncey*, *Galley Subtle*, *Anne Gallant*, *Morian of Danzig*, *Antelope*, *Henry Grace à Dieu* and the *Mary Rose* took pride of place. As you can see from Source C, this would have been a costly building programme.

With an array of potential invaders eager to make Britain their own, England needed a strong navy to protect herself and her commercial interests.

- What was the navy like?
- What was it like to serve on a warship such as the Mary Rose?

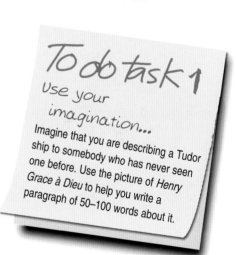

To do task 1

Use your imagination...

Imagine that you are describing a Tudor ship to somebody who has never seen one before. Use the picture of *Henry Grace à Dieu* to help you write a paragraph of 50–100 words about it.

Artist's impression of *Henry Grace à Dieu*: a large and expensive warship.

Source A — **Great Harry's Navy,** *Geoffrey Moorhouse, Orion, 2006*

"*Henry Grace à Dieu (by the Grace of God) was often as not known as the Great Harry. At 1,500 tons it was the biggest that the English would see for another 250 years.*"

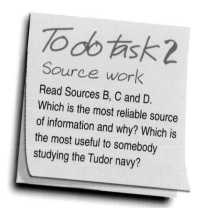

To do task 2

Source work

Read Sources B, C and D. Which is the most reliable source of information and why? Which is the most useful to somebody studying the Tudor navy?

NB

In case you are wondering, a fathom is 6ft, or 1.8m.

Leonardo da Vinci died in 1519.

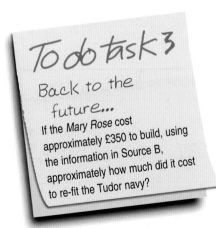

To do task 3

Back to the future...

If the Mary Rose cost approximately £350 to build, using the information in Source B, approximately how much did it cost to re-fit the Tudor navy?

Ivan the Terrible began his rule over Russia in 1547.

World Link

Source B — From the British Monarchy website

"Henry also invested in the navy, and increased its size from 5 to 53 ships (including the Mary Rose, *the remains of which lie in the Portsmouth Naval Museum)."*

Source C

From the *Guardian* newspaper website

"The ship was one of a pair recorded as costing £700 to build."

Life on board the boats

When men joined the navy in Tudor times, few knew what they were letting themselves in for. Life on board the boats was hard and the sailors were poorly paid. An alternative to navy service was to become a 'privateer' (a self-employed mercenary seaman), which for many was far more appealing. Sailors lived with the ever common risks of diseases such as scurvy, dysentery and sea sickness, and death by drowning.

Food was often short on long voyages and had to be carefully **rationed**. Records show that the sailors had access to salted meat and fish, ship's biscuits, fruit, butter, cheese and beer, among other things. However, some of the food, particularly the biscuits, was often infested with weevils and maggots.

The sailors were totally at the mercy of the weather, as modern weather forecasting equipment did not exist. They had to rely on the moon and stars to predict the tides and estimate their location. Sailors had to be constantly on the look-out for sandbanks and reefs. The depth of the sea would be checked by dropping a piece of rope with a lead on the end. The rope was pre-marked with measurement in fathoms. The plumbline, as it was called (like the one shown here) would remain the main way of measuring the depth of water for centuries. A later version had a larger metal weight on the end with a rough base which allowed sailors to find out what sort of material made up the seabed – mud, sand, stone and so on.

A plumb line.

Sailors had to be brave to climb high into a ship's rigging.

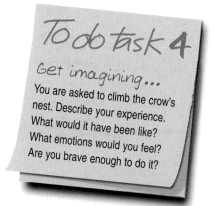

To do task 4

Get imagining...

You are asked to climb the crow's nest. Describe your experience. What would it have been like? What emotions would you feel? Are you brave enough to do it?

To do task 5

Get researching...

Use the internet to research the Mary Rose in more detail. Produce a Powerpoint presentation on the boat and its recovery from the Solent.

Rigging (adjusting) the sails meant **perilous** journeys high up into the ship's mast and ropes, and sometimes up into the crow's nest to look for land or enemy ships, even in stormy conditions when the boat was rolling wildly. The design of the Tudor **galleons** meant that in storms they lurched up and down violently, causing extreme seasickness.

The boats

Some of the boats were poorly designed (by today's standards) and took a long time to travel short distances, especially in rough weather. They depended on wind for power – they couldn't even get out of harbour if the wind and tide were against them. The shape of the boats, with high sterns (the back part of the boat), looked grand and impressive, and gave some protection to the deck, but also made the boats heavy and clumsy to move.

Source D **Great Harry's Navy,** *Geoffrey Moorhouse, Orion, 2006*

"The high sterns that were beginning to come into naval architecture were largely down to a fear of being pooped: of having a sea come in over the stern, at least sweeping away everything in its path, but more probably sinking the ship and its crew."

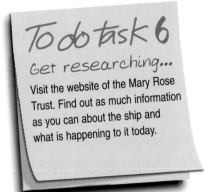
To do task 6
Get researching...
Visit the website of the Mary Rose Trust. Find out as much information as you can about the ship and what is happening to it today.

Stop the Clock
William Shakespeare was born in 1564.

BUZZ WORDZZ

Formidable
Galleons
Perilous
Rationed
Rigging

The *Mary Rose*

The *Mary Rose* takes pride of place in the history of the Tudor navy, not because it was the biggest or the finest, but because it is the only surviving Tudor warship in the world, although it did sink on 19 July 1545. This sinking preserved it, as warships were usually dismantled when they were no longer seaworthy, and their wood and other materials re-used.

The *Mary Rose* was built between 1509–11 and was named after Mary, Henry VIII's sister. The second part of the name is a reference to the Tudor Rose that was the symbol of the House of Tudor. The *Mary Rose* was the flagship (lead ship) of the navy. She was 126ft long, 43ft wide and 15ft tall. When fully loaded she weighed over 700 tons. This huge weight was largely because the main building materials for the *Mary Rose* were elm and oak, and she had an exceptionally heavy load of cannons.

As a heavily armed warship, the *Mary Rose* carried 77 cannons, and was one of the first ships to have gun-ports (openings in the side of the ship that the cannons could be fired through). Previously, most cannons had been fired from the top decks. The gun-ports were placed along the hull (the main body) of the ship, some of them being only 16in above the water level. Having the weight of the cannons low down in the ship did help to stabilise it, but also carried the risk of water flooding in if the gun-ports weren't securely closed.

Source E

Henry VIII: The King and Court,
Alison Weir, Pimlico, 2001

"In July 1545, French ships attacked the south coast. The King went down to Portsmouth to review his fleet and oversee operations. On the 19th, as the French lay off the Isle of Wight, Henry was standing on the battlements of Southsea Castle, watching the Great Harry lead his ships out of the Solent to do battle. Suddenly, the Mary Rose, with all hands on board, keeled over and sank. More than 600 men drowned, and their cries could be heard by the horrified King."

The preserved remains of the *Mary Rose* are on display in Portsmouth.

The sinking of the *Mary Rose*

France and England had been at war intermittently since the beginning of the Tudor period and the *Mary Rose* had been involved in many sea battles. When, in 1545, the French forces set out to invade Britain, they were met by the might of the English navy, including the *Mary Rose*.

Many suggestions have been made about why the boat sank. These have included:

 sudden changes in wind direction

 open gun-ports allowed water into the ship

 unruly men on board

 heavy guns made her unstable

 damage from French warships attacking her.

To do task 7

Get thinking...

Look at the possible reasons for the sinking of the *Mary Rose*. Outline each reason, with extra details why each one may have led to her sinking.

However, most historians now agree that it was the open gun-ports that were the downfall of the *Mary Rose*. As the ship turned into position against the French, water sloshed through the open gun-ports and caused her to sink. Not long before the battle, the gun-ports had been re-fitted and were positioned lower down on the ship. The risk of flooding had not been anticipated. The *Mary Rose* lay undisturbed at the bottom of the River Solent until she was re-discovered in 1836 and then finally raised from the seabed in

The moment, in October 1982, when the remains of the *Mary Rose* were lifted from the water, before being taken to the purpose-built museum in Portsmouth.

The Tudor navy was again called into battle, this time against the mighty Spanish empire during the reign of Henry VIII's daughter – Elizabeth I (1558–1603).

- Why was Spain a threat to England?
- How did the English defeat the Spanish Armada?

To do task 1
Comprehension

1. Which two famous English sailors stole from the Spanish?
2. Who was Philip of Spain married to?
3. Who led the Spanish Armada?

A portrait of King Philip of Spain.

Why did Spain want to attack England?

In the sixteenth century, Spain had a large empire of countries under its control. The ownership of such territory meant that the Spanish took advantage of any wealth or treasure (such as gold, spices and precious stones) found in these lands. This **'plunder'** was sent home to Spain by boat. The ships that carried this precious cargo were easy targets for English seamen, such as Sir Francis Drake (pictured here) and Sir John Hawkins, who stole it before it reached Spain. Drake, in particular, made a lot of money from this piracy. This stealing was only one of many reasons why Spain had a long-standing grievance with Queen Elizabeth I and the English. These attacks were not unbeknown to the Queen herself, who had given her official stamp of approval to them.

Sir Francis Drake.

Another major reason for the antagonism between the two countries came to a head in 1585, when the **Protestant** population in the Netherlands rebelled against Catholic Spanish rule. Elizabeth sent English troops to help the rebels, much to King Philip of Spain's annoyance. It was in England's interests to bolster the Netherlands, because Spanish control there meant they could attack England much more easily than from Spain.

Philip's eye on England

Philip had been married to England's former Queen, Mary, but the marriage was an unhappy one and they had no children. Philip had set his heart on the country rather than the woman and he encouraged Mary to build up England's already large navy even further. After Mary's death, Philip proposed to Elizabeth, who declined his advances. But this did not put Philip off his desire to rule England.

When Elizabeth had executed her relative, Mary, Queen of Scots, the Scottish monarch's claim to the throne of England had been passed on to Philip: a fellow Catholic.

Support in high places

Philip had the support of Pope Sixtus V (the head of the Catholic Church) in his quest to rule England. Many Catholics believed that because Elizabeth's father – Henry VIII – had not been officially allowed to divorce Catherine of Aragon: Elizabeth was illegitimate. Therefore she had no real claim to the throne of England.

If his planned invasion of England (which he finally attempted in 1588) was a success, Philip intended his own daughter to become Queen of England after he had removed Elizabeth from the throne.

A portrait of Queen Elizabeth I.

Girl power

Against this background of distrust, suspicion and rivalry, the Spanish threat to England was very real. Spain was a powerful, rich country with a lot of resources and a strong fighting fleet: the English navy was to be well and truly tested.

In 1588 the Spanish gathered forces to invade England, and Elizabeth spurred her troops on with a **rousing** speech (see Source A).

Source A **The History of Britain and Ireland,**

Mike Corbishley, John Gillingham, Rosemanry Kelly, Ian Dawson, James Mason and Kenneth O. Morgan, Oxford University Press, 2006

"I am resolved in the midst and heat of the battle to live or die amongst you all. ... I know I have the body of a weak and feeble woman, but I have the heart and stomach of a King, and the King of England too, and I think foul scorn that Parma, or Spain, or any Prince of Europe should dare to invade the borders of my realm."

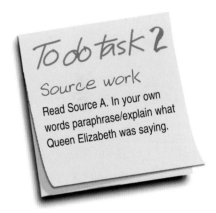

To do task 2
Source work
Read Source A. In your own words paraphrase/explain what Queen Elizabeth was saying.

The Spanish plan

Philip's only way to attack England, an island, was to send a fleet of ships. (Of course this was long, long before the invention of aircraft!) Preparations for the attack began in 1586, with Philip carefully organising and building up his fleet. The Spanish **Armada** (or fleet of warships) assembled in the Spanish harbour of Càdiz. However, the Spanish suffered a major set-back in their preparations when Francis Drake, sensing an opportunity to annoy everybody in Spain even further, attacked Càdiz in 1587 and set fire to a number of the Spanish ships. This attack by fire-ships on the Spanish fleet has been known historically as 'singeing the King of Spain's beard'.

The attack caused major delays for the Spanish, as Philip had to re-build his fleet. But a more important problem was that the Spanish commander – the Duke of Medina Sidonia – had no experience of naval warfare and even suffered from sea-sickness.

Philip's invasion of England finally began in May 1588. His plan was to sail from Spain up the English Channel to pick up extra soldiers from Calais and then from the Netherlands, before turning his invasion fleet towards England – his ultimate target. His Armada carried over 30,000 men but for the invasion to be successful more men were needed.

Map showing the location of Spain in relation to England and the route of the Spanish Armada.

N

Scotland

Ireland

Wales

England

Netherlands: collect more soldiers

Netherlands

Calais: pick up soldiers

France

Portugal

Spain

Càdiz

0   300 miles

To do task 3

Get creative...

You have been asked to plot the path of the Armada from Spain to the British Isles. Using your own knowledge and an atlas to help, write a report to show just what route the Spanish Armada took and why.

Most of the ships in the Armada were really designed as transport ships: built to carry large numbers of troops for land battles. Unlike the British ships, few were designed for warfare at sea. Philip hoped that the conflict would take place on English soil, rather than at sea, so his **priority** was to land thousands of troops on the coast of England as quickly as possible. He was even reluctant to make plans about what to do if the Spanish fleet was attacked before reaching England. He knew that Spain might not win a naval battle against the maritime power of England.

England's coastal defences were not strong. The castles built by Henry VIII more than 50 years previously would not be able to withstand Spanish cannon fire. English soldiers were recruited hastily in case of an invasion but they were poorly trained and badly equipped. If Philip was successful in landing Spanish troops in southern England, his chances of conquering the Kent countryside and moving forces up to London were very high indeed.

The fate of the Spanish Armada

7. Spanish ships flee for home.

8. Storms and bad weather cause difficulties for the Spanish all the way.

Scotland

Ireland

6. Running battles up the east coast.

Wales

England

4. The Armada is sighted by the English as it sails up the Channel.

Calais

5. Spanish anchor off Calais, due to collect more troops. The English fleet attacks.

France

Bay of Biscay

3. Resupply at Corunna then sail for Calais.

Corunna

Portugal

Lisbon

Spain

2. Resupply in Lisbon.

1. The Armada sets sail from Càdiz harbour.

Càdiz

Source C

From the National Maritime Museum website

"Sir Francis Drake was very active in the Armada battles of 1588. One of the most famous incidents involving Drake was when the Spanish flagship, the Rosario, collided with another ship. It lost its mast and became separated from the rest of the Spanish fleet. Drake captured it, even though he had been given the job of tracking the Armada with his stern lantern alight to guide all the other English ships following him. The prize of the Rosario must have been too difficult to resist. The ship was taken without a single shot being fired, still with the royal money chest on board."

To do task 4
Get creative...
You have been asked to produce an article on the Spanish Armada for a historical magazine. Use the information on pages 54–57 to produce this article, using no more than 300 words.

It was usual for important people to have their own 'seal' that was easily recognisable. This is the seal of Lord Howard.

Source B — Tudor War,
Peter Heppelwhite,
Hodder Headline, 2002

"In July 1588, the fearsome Spanish Armada set sail. The Catholic King Philip II of Spain had finally decided to crush Protestant England with a fleet of warships. The Spanish planned to sweep aside the English navy, pick up extra troops from Calais, and invade England, where they would crush the English militia. But it all went horribly wrong."

Once in England Philip hoped to use anti-Protestant feeling among the English Catholics to build up even more support for his cause.

Drake and Howard

The English navy was led by two far more capable campaigners than Medina Sidonia – Lord Howard of Effingham and the prestigious Sir Francis Drake.

Drake

Drake made no attempt to hide his dislike for the Spanish and, by the time Elizabeth was Queen, Drake was a well-known attacker of Spanish treasure ships. He gained enormous wealth from robbing ships of their gold, as well as giving many spoils to Elizabeth herself. He was an experienced, confident sailor and by the time the Spanish Armada arrived he was in his early forties having been born sometime between 1541 and 1543 (records are unclear).

Howard

Charles Howard was a relative of Queen Elizabeth I. Despite being made Lord Admiral in 1585, he was not a great sailor and did not have a huge amount of experience at sea. He was, though, a very talented leader of men and worked extraordinarily well with Drake, acknowledging his superior maritime expertise. By the time the Armada arrived, Howard was 52 years of age.

The fleets

Drake's fleet contained 130 boats, which were all ready for war at the time of the invasion. The English ships were fast and manoeuvrable, with powerful cannons that could fire over a long range and were **superior** to the Spanish weapons. The English ships sat lower in the water, which meant that the enemy's cannons often fired over the top of them. The Spanish had also removed many of their cannons while waiting for the new troops from the Spanish Netherlands and therefore lacked the necessary fire-power to compete with the English on even terms.

The invasion is on!

On 19 July 1588, the Spanish Armada sailed through the English Channel in a **crescent** formation, which the English could hardly fail to see. But Drake and Howard were initially powerless to attack: strong winds and tides kept the English ships in the harbour. One well-known tale from history has Drake watching the Spanish Armada sail by while he was playing a game of bowls on Plymouth green, happy knowing that nobody could accuse him of shirking his responsibilities.

Warning beacons were lit along the coastline of England as the Armada sailed past. When the English finally managed to get out of the harbour they chased the Spanish up the Channel.

A fatal mistake

At this point Medina Sidona made a fatal decision. On 27 July he gave orders for the Spanish ships to anchor just off Calais. The troops were to rest and the Duke hoped to build up his forces and stocks of ammunition. The English, though, saw an opportunity to take advantage and sent fire-ships into the middle of the Spanish crescent-shaped formation of ships. The Spanish panicked and the ships could not keep their protective formation. They were forced to dash back into the English Channel, where they were again attacked by the waiting English.

Bad luck Spanish

By 29 July both fleets had sailed out of the English Channel and up the east coast of England, and were locked in battle at Gravelines, off the Netherlands' coast. The English blocked the way back home for the Spanish, who were therefore forced to head around Scotland then down the coast of Ireland in order to return home. Bad luck hit the Spanish when a strong storm whipped up. Forty-four Spanish boats were smashed on the rocky Irish coastline and sank.

The defeat of the Spanish Armada raised Elizabeth I's popularity and proved that England was a dangerous enemy. In contrast, Philip was heavily criticised for his role in the attack and Spanish ships never attempted another invasion of England.

This painting, of part of the Armada in battle with Drake, was painted a long time after the battle took place. Does that make it unreliable as a source?

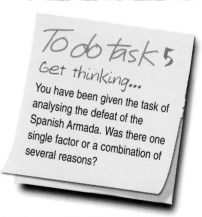

Discussion POINT

Is it right to invade another country over the issue of religion?

To do task 5

Get thinking...

You have been given the task of analysing the defeat of the Spanish Armada. Was there one single factor or a combination of several reasons?

BUZZ WORDZZ

Armada
Crescent
Plunder
Priority
Protestant
Rousing
Superior

Stop the Clock

Portugal was not independent of Spain until 1640.

A civil war is a war between two sides of the same country. Civil wars began in England in 1640 and ended in 1651, when Charles II was crowned King of England.

- Why did the Civil Wars happen?
  - Who won?
  - What were the consequences?

Why were they fought?

The King involved in the English Civil Wars was Charles Stuart (Charles I of England and Scotland). He was a controversial monarch, whose rule was never without incident (see Book 3 *Rule Makers & Rule Breakers*). He managed to annoy a large proportion of his subjects, including those living in Scotland.

Charles had a particularly difficult relationship with Parliament. Between 1629 and 1640 Charles ruled entirely without their input. This was because he disliked handing responsibility over to them, preferring to rule independently. When he did eventually recall Parliament he kept dissolving (getting rid of) the assembly when they refused to give him more money. Money was something that Charles needed desperately for many reasons.

Source A — **The English Civil War,** *Maurice Ashley, Sutton Publishing, 1992*

"Though one speaks (correctly) of the English revolution and the English Civil Wars, one has to remember that, politically at least, two occurrences that led to the conflict in England were the vain attempt by Charles I to suppress in 1639 and 1640 risings by his Scottish subjects, compelling him after an interval of eleven years to recall an English Parliament to ask it for financial aid [money], and the Irish rebellion which broke out in the autumn of 1641, sparking off Civil Wars through an argument about which side was to control the English armed forces recruited to suppress it. Thus rebellions in Scotland and Ireland gave rise to Civil Wars in a country with a much larger population."

Woodcut illustrations depicting the brutal repression of rebellions in Ireland in 1641.

To do task 1
Comprehension
1. When did Charles rule entirely without Parliament?
2. What was 'ship money'?
3. What was a 'tithe'?

To do task 2
Source work
What does Source A tell you about the underlying causes of the English Civil Wars? Is it a reliable source?

Charles' need for money for wars, himself or his kingdom, was a constant source of argument between him and **Parliament**. He was always short of money, partly because he loved spending money that he didn't have. To pay for his lavish lifestyle he had to sell off valuable land and assets, and what land he did have left brought in a very low income. As well as this **extravagant** spending, Charles needed money to pay for another war with Spain. So what was he to do?

Tax, tax, tax!

He had no option but to levy taxes on the people of England. This caused huge resentment, as everyone already paid heavy taxes to the Church and landowners, which were known as 'tithes' and represented one-tenth of the income of these people. Tithes that had been purchased

A portrait of Charles I

by private individuals, which still had to be paid, were known as 'impropriations'.

These, along with other taxes that had to be paid during religious services such as marriages and for the upkeep of the clergy, also caused widespread ill-feeling, as did the misuse of power by the Church courts.

As well as these taxes, Charles asked the people to pay two more taxes that were universally disliked.

Ship money – this tax had traditionally financed the Royal Navy and was usually only paid by the people who lived on the coast in times of absolute necessity (usually when pirates threatened the coastline). However, in 1635, Charles decided that everyone should pay it and thus raise a lot more money. Between 1637 and 1640 it raised Charles an extra £750,000. The tax was eventually made illegal by Parliament in 1641.

'Stuart' money was often being taken away from people far too easily by Charles I. The reverse of the coins says 'EXURGAT DEUS DISSIPENTUR INIMICI' ('Let God arise and His enemies be scattered').

Source B

From the Open2.net website

"King Charles I had the misfortune of ascending the throne at a time when Crown–Parliament relations were becoming increasingly tense, and when religious antagonisms (at home and abroad) were growing in volatility. Only an extremely flexible and imaginative monarch could hope to steer the ship of state through these dangers, but Charles' behaviour and strategy indicated a singular lack of such qualities."

NB
£750,000 in 1640 is thought to be the equivalent of around £75,000,000 in today's money, although estimates of this kind are notoriously unreliable.

To do task 3
Get thinking…
Use the information on pages 58–61 to outline the reasons why civil war broke out. You may wish to do this in written paragraphs, by using bullet points or in a spider diagram.

Tonnage and poundage – This hated tax was imposed on wine, imports and exports. One 'ton' was a measurement of wine – a ton of wine. Poundage was a tax on imported and exported goods, paid against each pound (lb) in weight of goods (1lb is roughly the same as 450g). The right to claim this tax had been granted to Kings and Queens in 1414 and, in the eyes of the law, the King was allowed to claim it for life. However, Parliament had only granted Charles the right to collect tonnage and poundage for one year in 1625 and for two months in 1641. Charles was not happy about this attempt to ration what he saw as his right.

The issue of religion

Another issue that annoyed many English was the marriage of the King to a Catholic French princess: Henrietta Maria. To the Protestant people of England this looked as though the King was becoming more sympathetic towards 'Popery' (**Catholicism**) and they weren't happy about this. At one point Parliament had threatened to impeach (remove from rule legally, using force) Henrietta Maria and in retaliation, on 4 January 1642, Charles tried to arrest five members of Parliament and charge them with treason.

Yet more controversy had been created by Archbishop Laud deciding to replace the wooden altar tables in the churches with stone tables (a traditional Catholic element), which was seen as a hint that he might want to bring back the Catholic religion. Laud's decision to impose the **Anglican** prayer book on the Scottish Church also caused much dissatisfaction.

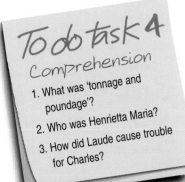

The Anglican Prayer Book, also known as the English 'Common Prayer Book'.

A portrait of Charles I's wife, Henrietta Maria.

To do task 4

Comprehension

1. What was 'tonnage and poundage'?
2. Who was Henrietta Maria?
3. How did Laude cause trouble for Charles?

Factors of war

Wars do not break out without reason, and usually there are several factors that build up over time. As you can now see, all these factors combined with the growing tension between Parliament and the King, resulting in the outbreak of civil war.

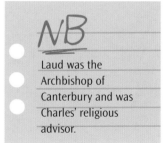

NB

Laud was the Archbishop of Canterbury and was Charles' religious advisor.

Archbishop Laud.

The divide within England

The Civil Wars meant that England was divided by loyalty to either the King or Parliament. However, this did not split the population neatly down the middle. It would be logical to think of the common man siding with Parliament, and the nobility and the gentry taking the side of the King, but that was not always the case. Neither was it a north/south divide (north for the King and south for Parliament). In reality, people from all levels of society and from different parts of the country chose to fight for either King or Parliament (see Source C).

Source C — From the National Portrait Gallery website

"The son of a Reading draper, Laud prospered under the patronage of the Duke of Buckingham and was appointed Archbishop of Canterbury in 1633. He supported the political and religious policies of Charles I and carried out Strafford's policy of 'Thorough' in ecclesiastical affairs, working for uniformity of doctrine and practice. His attempt to impose uniformity on the church provoked armed resistance in Scotland. Parliament impeached and imprisoned him in 1640–1 and he was beheaded in 1645."

The wars even divided some families in their loyalty to either the King or Parliament. Generally, however, the divide was religious: Puritans supported Parliament, while Anglicans and Catholics often pledged their allegiance to the King. Some historians also believe that people fought on the side of whichever army happened to be nearest them, dropping their allegiance when the fighting moved on.

Source D — From Howard's Potted History of the English Civil War

"Families became divided on a matter of principle, whilst towns and villages found themselves in 'no-man's land' between rival garrisons, both likely to come seeking 'voluntary' contributions, in money, provisions or both."

Who was stronger?

Both armies were similar in size. The only major difference was that the Royalist (King's) army had more horses and cavalrymen and Parliament had slightly more infantry. Because of the numbers of **cavalry**, the Royalist army gained the nickname 'Cavaliers'. The name Cavalier is derived from the Spanish name for horsemen: *cavalieros*. The Parliamentarian army gained the nickname 'Roundheads' because of the short haircuts that some of the younger troops had.

Roundhead (left) and Cavalier (right) troopers, in typical uniform of the Civil Wars.

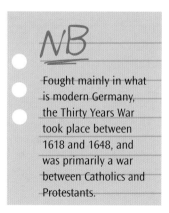

To do task 5

Get creative...

Design a recruitment poster for the New Model Army. Think about what sort of man you want to recruit and remember what Source G reports what Cromwell said about the ideal man for his army.

Both sides were fairly evenly matched in terms of numbers of troops, each side with around 13,000 men at their disposal. The Royalist army contained troops from Germany and Holland, as well as those from England. It relied heavily on paid professionals – called **mercenaries**. Throughout the conflict, the King's army was forever dwindling in numbers and repeatedly needed topping up.

Parliament had the support of the navy as well as its 'recruited' army. Ship Money had back-fired on Charles again, as the sailors decided that they would rather fight against their King than for him. Unlike the Royalist army, most of Parliament's army were English.

Who was Prince Rupert?

The military leader of the Royalist forces was Prince Rupert. He was born on 17 December 1619 in Prague and went by the titles of Count Palatine of the Rhine or Prince Rupert of the Rhine. His uncle was the King himself: Charles. Well educated, Rupert could speak many European languages and was a strong-willed man.

Rupert's background in warfare had been forged in the Thirty Years War (1618–48). He had a reputation for being arrogant and was unwilling to take advice from anybody but the King. On the battlefield he presented a strange image by carrying his dog, called Boy, into battle with him.

Source E — From the website of the Royal Armouries

"Prince Rupert, was a veteran of the Thirty Years War. His cavalry charge at Powick Bridge gave him the reputation of a hero and his dog Boy was seen as a magical familiar. After Marston Moor though, Rupert hid in a bean field and Boy was shot."

NB

Fought mainly in what is modern Germany, the Thirty Years War took place between 1618 and 1648, and was primarily a war between Catholics and Protestants.

A portrait of Prince Rupert, leader of the pro-monarch Royalist forces in the Civil Wars.

Who were Fairfax and Cromwell?

The two men who led the armies of Parliament were Thomas Fairfax (Black Tom) and Oliver Cromwell. Fairfax was born on 17 January 1612 in Yorkshire and was a renowned fighter who was extremely brave. Cromwell was born on 25 April 1599 and was the Member of Parliament (MP) for Huntingdon. Cromwell was a '**Radical**' Puritan (a Puritan was a strict and devout Protestant in the sixteenth and seventeenth centuries). He had worked his way up to the rank of Lieutenant General commanding his own cavalry regiment, which was nicknamed the 'Ironsides'.

The New Model Army

The most famous fighting force of the English Civil Wars was Parliament's New Model Army. Cromwell decided to choose his own soldiers, so that he could pick men who were suitable for conflict, rather than those who had just entered the army because of family tradition, money or status. Cromwell believed in ability rather than privilege (see Sources F and G).

A portrait of Oliver Cromwell.

A portrait of Thomas Fairfax.

NB

It was called the New Model Army because it was a national, not a regional, army that could move around the whole of the country if needed.

To do task 6
Get researching...
Research Oliver Cromwell in more detail. What sort of man was he? Produce a 'who's who' contribution on him.

Source F — The Autobiography of the British Soldier,

John Lewis-Stempel,
Headline Review, 2007

"In April 1645, at Cromwell's urging, the flagging militias [bands of men] of Parliament were replaced by a professional, trained army. One, moreover, that was paid properly, out of taxation. And so, Britain's first standing army was born. Numbering some 22,000 men, the 'New Model Army' was Cromwell's 'ironside' division writ large."

Source G

The History of Britain and Ireland,

Mike Corbishley, John Gillingham, Rosemanry Kelly, Ian Dawson, James Mason and Kenneth O. Morgan,
Oxford University Press, 2006

"Cromwell said: 'I had rather have a plain russet-coated Captain that knows what he fights for and loves what he knows, than what you call a gentleman and is nothing else. ... If you choose Godly, honest men to be captains of horse, honest men will follow them.'"

BUZZ WORDZZ

Anglican
Catholicism
Cavalry
Mercenaries
Parliament
Radical

Fighting conditions

Life as a soldier during the English Civil Wars was difficult. Soldiers regularly faced death, terrible injury, disease or illness. Many soldiers were struck down by typhus or camp fever before they had even drawn their weapons. The weapons ranged from swords, muskets and pikes to cannons and mortars. Many of the men who fought were not highly trained. It was, for many, their first experience of warfare. Pitted against and alongside highly trained foreign soldiers, their greatest challenge was simply to stay alive.

The battles

As in most wars of the seventeenth century, the English Civil Wars was not one continuous war, like more modern conflicts such as World War II, but a series of battles fought over several years. Armies were difficult to move, roads were often bad and mobility was affected by the weather. There were long periods when no fighting took place: the armies needed time to re-equip themselves and to travel.

The battles of the English Civil Wars were fought all over the country. The most significant battles are shown on the maps on the left.

By 1646 Charles and the Royalists were defeated and the King fled to Scotland: the kingdom that he ruled alongside England. He expected to receive sympathy and refuge, but the Scottish sold him to the Parliamentary forces.

The effects of the wars

Execution

On 30 January 1649 King Charles I was executed by Parliament. It was unprecedented in England to kill a monarch, and the event was extremely controversial. Many people believed that the Parliamentarians had gone too far (see Source H).

Royalist

Parliamentarian

These maps show how the Civil Wars unfolded territorially.

To do task 7

Source work

What do Sources H and J suggest about the general feelings towards the wars and the execution of the King? Are they reliable sources?

Source H — **Charles I's Execution,** from the Historic Royal Palaces, website

"A groan as I never heard before, and desire I may never hear again went up from the crowd watching the unimaginable event – the killing of the Lord's anointed sovereign.

This realisation and the dignity with which the King conducted himself on the scaffold created a great wave of emotion for the dead monarch. Charles I was recognised as a martyr and 30 January was remembered as Charles the Martyr day."

Subsequently, there would be no crowned monarch in England until the return of Charles' son, Charles II, from exile in 1660.

With the death of Charles I, England was ruled by Parliament, but in 1653 Cromwell dissolved it and declared himself Lord Protector of England.

Expense

The Civil Wars had a huge financial impact on English people. They were obliged to pay taxes to finance both sides, including equipping the troops and feeding them. They were also forced to 'billet' the troops in their own homes. Some people formed their own local small armies to fight off the demands of both the Royalist and Parliamentarian forces. There was widespread fear that law and order would break down completely.

Source J — The English Civil War, Maurice Ashley, Sutton Publishing, 1992

"The New Model Army, which for the past two years had been marching about England destroying property and living on 'free quarter' was naturally unpopular with civilians. Petitions were dispatched to Parliament asking for its prompt disbandment."

Did people actually care about what was happening?

Some historians believe that there was little real interest among the people about who won the Civil Wars, provided that their lives did not change beyond recognition and that many were very reluctant to participate at all. Others believe that it had a large effect on the people of England. History is full of varying interpretations about the same event. Individual beliefs can only be based on the evidence that is available. So what do you think about the impact of the English Civil Wars?

Source K — The Civil Wars 1640–49, Angela Anderson, Hodder & Stoughton, 1999

"The Civil Wars was an enormous shock and upheaval for those involved in it, and it is important not to underestimate the fear and horror with which such an event would be regarded."

Source I

Why Did People Want the King Back in 1646?
From The National Archive's website

"Historians think that about 180,000 people died from fighting, accidents and disease. That was about 3.6% of the population. (In World War 1 around 2.6% of the population died.) The Civil War also saw terrible events. For example, in May 1644 Royalists massacred the Parliament forces in Bolton. This was provoked by the Parliament troops hanging several Royalist prisoners during the battle."

To do task 8
Source work
Read Sources I and K. Is it fair to compare the English Civil Wars with World War I?

Stop the Clock
The Great Russian Tsar, Peter the Great began his rule in 1682.

Introduction

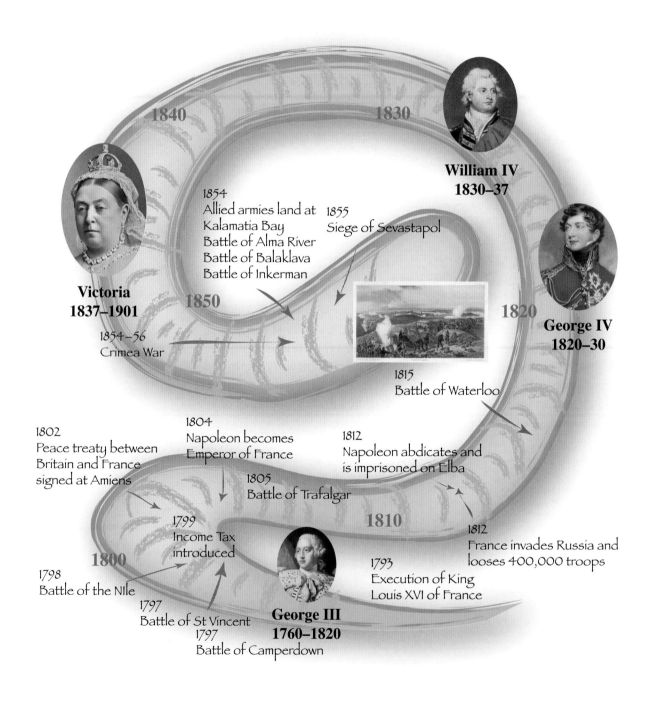

Who ruled?

1840

1830

**William IV
1830–37**

1854
Allied armies land at
Kalamatia Bay
Battle of Alma River
Battle of Balaklava
Battle of Inkerman

1855
Siege of Sevastapol

**Victoria
1837–1901**

1850

1820

**George IV
1820–30**

1854–56
Crimea War

1815
Battle of Waterloo

1802
Peace treaty between
Britain and France
signed at Amiens

1804
Napoleon becomes
Emperor of France

1812
Napoleon abdicates and
is imprisoned on Elba

1805
Battle of Trafalgar

1799
Income Tax
introduced

1810

1812
France invades Russia and
looses 400,000 troops

1800

1798
Battle of the Nile

1793
Execution of King
Louis XVI of France

1797
Battle of St Vincent

1797
Battle of Camperdown

**George III
1760–1820**

In the last chapter we looked at the English Civil Wars and their impact. In this chapter we move forward and look at a conflict that took place nearly 150 years later. So why have we made such a leap? It is not because the conflicts in between these two periods were unimportant, but rather that there is only so much room in every history book! Look at the map on this page. Which wars were fought between the Stuart periods and the Industrial Revolution that are not included in this book? Use the information to find out the basic facts about them, and then fill in the gaps in your knowledge by either asking your teacher, or doing some individual research. Then fill in the missing details on the map – names of countries, continents, important cities. What do you learn from the map about the extent and coverage of these conflicts?

Seven Years War

1756–63

Fought between Britain and Prussia, versus Russia, Sweden, Austria, France and Saxony.

Often referred to as the first truly 'world' war, because it was the first conflict to be fought around the world. Estimated deaths from the war range between 1 and 1.5 million.

The ending of the war paved the way for British dominance of India as French power there was effectively removed.

American War of Independence

1775–83

Also known as the American Revolutionary War. It began as a conflict between Britain and former colonies in America, but ended as a global war between European great powers.

Britain used naval superiority to capture coastal areas, but with a relatively small land army was unable to control the interior of the country.

Total deaths in the conflict are not known, but it is likely that more people involved died from disease than from actual combat. The huge costs of the war caused difficulties for all nations involved for years afterwards, and directly contributed to the French Revolution of 1789.

Dutch wars

1st Dutch War 1652–54
2nd Dutch War 1665–67
3rd Dutch War 1672–74

Known as the Dutch Wars in Britain, and as the English Wars in the Netherlands.

The fighting was largely about gaining control of valuable ocean trading routes.

The wars saw a huge growth in warship design and building by both sides.

By the early eighteenth century, Britain faced a new enemy in Europe – Napoleon Bonaparte. The French leader was building an empire across much of Europe and Britain's security was threatened.

- Why did he threaten Britain?
- How was he defeated?

A painting, created some time after the event took place, showing the ill-fated Louis XVI being seized by the mob.

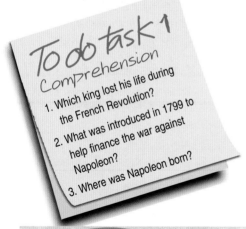

To do task 1
Comprehension

1. Which king lost his life during the French Revolution?
2. What was introduced in 1799 to help finance the war against Napoleon?
3. Where was Napoleon born?

Why was Britain at war with France?

In the late eighteenth century, France experienced an increase in popular protest and the people rose up against their king. In 1793 the French **Revolution** led to the **execution** of King Louis XVI, and France soon became a republic. At that time there was great competition for the vast trade networks that existed throughout Europe. Both Britain and France vied for control of these lucrative trade routes. When France took control of the Austrian Netherlands, Britain joined forces with other European countries to challenge the power of the French army. War was declared in 1793 – few people realised it would last over 20 years!

The **expansionist** tactics of the growing French empire (and her allies) brought French forces into conflict with Britain many times over the first decade of these wars. Three of the most significant battles were: the Battle of Camperdown, 1797, in which the British defeated the Dutch (who were allied to France); the Battle of Cape St Vincent, 1797, where the British defeated the Spanish fleet (who were allied to France); and the Battle of the Nile, 1798, where a young English naval commander, Horatio Nelson, successfully confronted the French fleet off the coast of Egypt.

Source A — Napoleonic Era, from The History Channel website

"The burden of taxes was increased and, more importantly, their collection was made much more effective. Taxes were mainly on property and income, with the main burden falling on the peasantry. However, despite his efforts, Napoleon was never able to create a surplus in the government's account because of his constant warfare across Europe."

Who won?

During these years, although individual battles were lost and won, neither side achieved decisive victory; the power struggle for **supremacy** in Europe and on the seas continued.

The war was expensive for all involved. The British people were taxed heavily to finance the continuation of the war, with income tax being introduced in 1799. Similar effects were experienced in France, as highlighted in Source A.

The constant need for money and resources took a heavy toll on the countries' finances, and military and naval forces became exhausted. This was the reason why, in 1802, a peace treaty between Britain and France was signed at Amiens. Both countries agreed to return some recently conquered territories and open up their trade again. However, the peace did not last and by 1803 they were at war again. The French united with Spain, increasing its naval strength, which was to pose the greatest challenge to Britain yet. The leader of the French forces and French nation was Napoleon Bonaparte.

To do task 2
Get thinking...
Using the information on this page, write a biography of Napoleon.

So who was Napoleon?

A portrait of Napoleon, dressed in full ceremonial uniform.

Source B

History: The Definitive Visual Guide,
Adam Hart-Davis, Dorling Kindersley, 2007

"The future French Emperor Napoleon Bonaparte was born Napoleone Buonaparte, a member of a poor Corsican noble family of Italian origin. A wild island of bandits and vendettas, Corsica became a part of France in 1768, the year before Napoleon's birth. When he was nine years old Napoleon attended school at Brienne le Château in France but he always spoke with a strong Italian accent. His family was poor enough to have his school fees paid by the state."

Napoleon had become a military commander through action in Egypt and at the Battle of the Nile. He was an expert in military tactics and could apply himself to most situations. In 1804 Napoleon became Emperor of France and its empire. He ruled over 70 million people. His power was unquestioned.

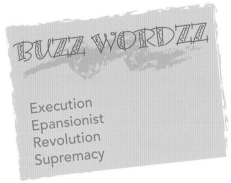

BUZZ WORDZZ

Execution
Epansionist
Revolution
Supremacy

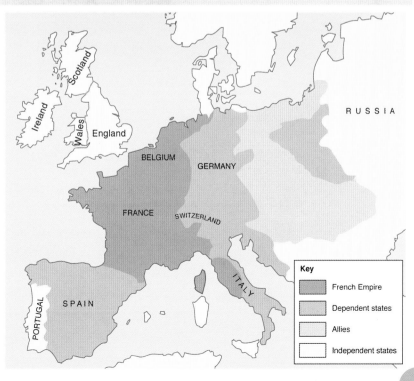

Map showing the extent of the French Empire in 1804.

Key
- French Empire
- Dependent states
- Allies
- Independent states

To do task 3

Get creative...

Design a poster warning people about the threat of invasion from Napoleon. You may want to use Sources B, C and D as inspiration.

Invasion planned

By 1803, the threat of Napoleon and his French forces invading Britain was very real. Napoleon's army now numbered around 130,000 men. French troops began to assemble along the French coast, with only the English Channel lying between Napoleon's forces and Britain. As well as the troops, Napoleon gathered a fleet of over 2,000 ships, positioned in ports along the coast. These were for the transport of **artillery**, men and horses.

Source C

Trafalgar, *Roy Adkins, Abacus, 2005*

"Over 100,000 troops were gradually concentrated in camps spread along 75 miles of French coastline around Calais and Boulogne. Many of the camps were plainly visible from the cliffs of Dover, causing a rising tide of panic in Southern England."

A Martello tower, seen as it looks today on the Suffolk coast.

In response, the British began to strengthen their coastal defences and build massive stuctures called Martello towers. In total, 73 of these forts and strongholds were built.

A lot was at stake. Naval power and control of the seas meant virtual world domination for the nation that managed them. At this time Britain controlled the seas but, as Napoleon's army became stronger in Europe, France gained territory, men and resources. Britain's own territory, power and wealth were under threat. The greatest weapon that Britain had against Napoleon and invasion was her navy. Only this could keep Napoleon at bay.

BUZZ WORDZZ

Administration
Artillery
Blockaded
Stranglehold

Source D — Voices from the Battle of Trafalgar, *Peter Warwick, David & Charles, 2005*

"Napoleon became the very personification of the people's fears. He was epitomized as the incarnation of evil. Wives and daughters would be ravished, and children were warned that 'the bogeyman' would take them away if they did not behave. Before these fears could be realized, however, Napoleon had to create a Grande Armée, a flotilla of boats to transport it and its materiel to England's shores, and a strategy for clearing the Channel of the Royal Navy. 'Let us be masters of the Straits but for six hours, and we shall be masters of the world' Napoleon declared in July 1804."

NB

A blockade is usually a military (or naval) attempt to prevent vital supplies from reaching an enemy by sea. Harbours and trade routes can both be blockaded, and ships carrying supplies either captured or sunk.

In an effort to prevent invasion, Britain began to blockade the French ports. When Spain became allied to France in 1804, Britain also **blockaded** Spanish ports. The aim of these blockades was to put a **stranglehold** on trade, so that much-needed money to finance Napoleon's forces was restricted.

Discussion POINT?

What is more important to Britain: the army or the navy?

Getting the ships together

Despite Britain's reputation as having a magnificent navy, by 1804 it was not in an adequate condition to fight. Lord St Vincent was First Lord of the Admiralty from 1801 to 1804, and during those years investment in the navy had deteriorated. He had dismissed many people working in naval dockyards and supplies were running very low. His successor, Lord Melville, inherited a navy that was in dire straits.

To do task 4

Source work

Read Source D. What does the source suggest about Napoleon? Is it a reliable point of view?

Source E **Trafalgar: The Long-term Impact,**
from the BBC website

"In three years as First Lord of the Admiralty, from 1801 to 1804, the megalomaniac Lord St Vincent had done as much as one man could to wreck British sea power.

Obsessed with a nightmare vision of corruption which scarcely existed outside his own imagination, he had paralysed naval administration, emptied the storehouses, and dismissed a large fraction of the dockyard workforce. In 1804 his successor, Lord Melville, calculated that he had 81 ships of the line in commission, of which 18 were fit only for home waters, and none of the remainder had an estimated service life remaining of more than five years. When Spain entered the war, in December 1804, Napoleon had over 100 ships of the line available."

To do task 5

Get thinking...

Using Source E, describe what was wrong with the British Navy in 1845.

It was vital that the British navy was in good condition.

Faced with the increasing threat across the English Channel, Lord Melville speeded up the repairs and re-organised the **administration** of the navy, which had become chaotic and inefficient. Fortunately, the skill and training of the British seamen, particularly the officers, remained high.

There were 32 British ships in total in the Royal Navy, of which *HMS Victory* was the flagship. Other boats included the *Colossus, Neptune, Britannia, Euralyus, Ajax, Mars, Agamemnon, Orion, Dreadnought, Spartiate, Defiance, Naiad, Prince, Phoebe* and *Pickle*.

Getting the men together

The ordinary seamen who served in the navy were either volunteers or were 'pressed' into service.

Source F — Life in Nelson's Navy,
Dudley Pope, Chatham Publishing, 1997

"The word 'press' was a corruption, in regular use by this war. The organisation at the ports was called the 'Impress Service' and the group of men under an officer was called a press gang, but the words were originally 'prest' and 'imprest'. Thus a man paid the King's shilling became an imprest, or prest, man, and in an age when spelling was not standardised eventually became 'pressed'."

The press gangs employed many different methods to 'press' people into service. Quite simply they had to transfer the King's shilling into the possession of the person that they wanted to serve in the navy.

Source G

The History of Britain and Ireland,
Mike Corbishley, John Gillingham, Rosemary Kelly, Ian Dawson, James Mason and Kenneth O. Morgan, Oxford University Press, 2006

"Ships' captains kept discipline by flogging sailors with the cat o' nine tails. Sailors died beneath hundreds of lashes, but lack of fresh water and sanitation meant that disease, rather than cannonballs, killed eighty percent of the casualties in the navy. Over half the crews were conscripts. Each town had to supply its quota of men and they frequently sent, according to Admiral Collingwood, 'the refuse of the gallows and the purgings of the gaol'."

This could be done by putting it in their pocket when they weren't watching, or dropping the coin into the bottom of a **tankard** that the man was drinking out of. Whatever method was used, it meant that the person was destined to serve a long time in the navy.

To do task 6
Get imagining...
Imagine that you have been press ganged. Use the information on pages 72 and 73 to write a letter home, explaining what you have had to go through.

Conditions on board the ships

Conditions on board the ships were hard to bear. There was very little space for the seamen who lived below deck, not much light, certainly no privacy and very little comfort.

Food

All food on board had to be preserved in salt or spices so it would last while sailors were at sea. The only fresh food that they had would be at the very beginning of a voyage or when they stopped at ports. This poor diet meant that sailors were prone to diseases caused by lack of nutrition and vitamins. To protect themselves against **scurvy** (a lack of vitamin C, which makes the skin flake and bleed) the sailors drank lime juice and became known as limeys or 'lime juicers'.

Source H — Life in Nelson's Navy, *Dudley Pope, Chatham Publishing, 1997*

"By the time the meat was cooked it might weigh a quarter less, but the cook would have a bucket full of the slush. He had in fact been skimming money off the water, because the seamen were only too anxious to buy the slush to spread on their bread, the name given to the coarse biscuit – the source of so many stories about weevils."

BUZZ WORDZZ

Scurvy
Tankard

To do task 7
Use the information in Source F on page 72 to write a 'children's dictionary' definition of the words press and impress.

With no fresh water, sailors were given regular rum rations which helped to keep out the cold and relieved the boredom of the job. Drunkenness was frequent among sailors.

Weapons

The ships were well stocked with the necessary weaponry. As well as the traditional weapons that were used on the battlefield (such as swivel guns, muskets and pistols), sailors also had tomahawks. These were axes that could be used to climb up the side of enemy vessels, but were also good for hand-to-hand fighting. All the boats were equipped with cannons that could fire standard cannon balls, chain and link shot – designed to bring down sails and rigging – and grape shot that would rip holes in the ships and sailors. Finally they were ready to take on the French and Napoleon.

Top: grape shot
Centre: cannon ball
Bottom: chain and link shot.

The Battle of Trafalgar, 1805, is one of the major events in British history.

- Why was it so important?
- Who won and why?

Source B

Voices from the Battle of Trafalgar,

Peter Warwick, David & Charles, 2005

"Nelson had been born 46 years earlier on 29th September 1758 at Burnham Thorpe in north Norfolk. His father was rector of the parish and his background was lower middle class. There were seven other children in his family."

The location of the Battle of Trafalgar. ▶

A portrait of Admiral Viscount Nelson.

Why was there a sea battle at Trafalgar?

When the two forces finally met at sea, it was after a long wait. Although the delay had given the British time to prepare, it had also led to boredom and frustration among the members of the navy.

Source A

The History of Britain and Ireland,

Mike Corbishley, John Gillingham, Rosemary Kelly, Ian Dawson, James Mason and Kenneth O. Morgan, Oxford University Press, 2006

"By 1803 the poor sailors had been at sea for the best part of two years waiting for Napoleon to invade. … The Government of the time was so concerned about the threat of invasion that they were even prepared to evacuate people to safer areas and had given local people weapons with which to defend themselves if the need arose."

By August 1805, the combined French and Spanish fleets were in the Spanish port of Cádiz. They were always under surveillance from British ships, so when the commander of the combined French and Spanish fleet, Villeneuve, finally left Cádiz on 18 October with 33 of his ships, the British quickly called for reinforcements. They were led by a national hero, Horatio Nelson, who set out in pursuit of Villeneuve.

At first, Nelson kept his fleet of 27 ships out of the sight of the enemy, but by 21 October he was closing in on the enemy fleet off the Cape of Trafalgar, near the Strait of Gibraltar.

Nelson

Admiral Viscount Nelson was an experienced naval campaigner. Known as a kind and inspiring leader, Nelson had the respect of all his sailors. His outstanding skills in naval strategy even gained him the respect of his enemy, Napoleon, who kept a bust of him in his private rooms!

The battle

Nelson's key battle strategy was to destroy the enemy flagship, which he rightly assumed would then leave the rest of the enemy fleet in chaos. After five hours of fierce fighting, 19 French and Spanish ships either had been destroyed or had surrendered. Nelson's flagship, *Victory*, delivered the decisive blow.

Source C

Battle of Trafalgar,
from the National Archive's website

"At around midday, off Cape Trafalgar, Nelson's fleet formed into two columns. One was led by Nelson in HMS Victory, *the other by Collingwood, in HMS* Royal Sovereign. *They sailed towards a single line of 33 French and Spanish ships on which served nearly 30,000 men. Nelson was intent on concentrating his ships' attack on breaking the enemy line at several strategic points, a tactic which would surprise the enemy and causing what he referred to as a 'pell-mell battle'. This would favour the superior gunnery and seamanship of the British fleet. The tactic was dangerous as the leading ships of the two British divisions were raked head-on with enemy gunfire from about noon without being able to return fire until they closed in on the enemy line, as HMS* Victory *did at about 12:30. Nelson had instructed his officers that if anything should go wrong with his plan and 'in case signals can neither be seen or perfectly understood, no captain can do very wrong if he places his ship alongside that of the enemy'."*

The battle ended as a crushing defeat for Villeneuve, but Britain's hero died in his flagship. He was shot by a French sniper and was hit by a musket ball through the shoulder: he died from his wounds. As well as Nelson, in total the British lost around 1,700 men and the French and Spanish around 5,000.

The Battle of Trafalgar was significant for two main reasons: firstly it stopped the threat of a French invasion of Britain; and, secondly, it re-established Britain's naval supremacy.

Discussion POINT ?

How important is it to have a good leader?

Source D

The Battle of Trafalgar,
Andrew Lambert, from the BBC website

"Soon afterwards the Victory *ran right under the stern of the French flagship, the* Bucentaure, *and fired a double shotted broadside that made the enemy ship shudder, and killed or wounded over 200 men. Admiral Villeneuve was the only man left standing on the quarter deck. Villeneuve was trapped on a crippled ship, and the Franco-Spanish centre was reduced to chaos, lacking the leadership to meet the irresistible British."*

To do task 1
Source work

Use Sources C and D to piece together what happened in the last phases of the battle. What do they tell us about the tactics of the British and why do you think they used these particular tactics?

Many ships were wrecked in the fighting.

Napoleon had already tasted defeat in the wars against Britain. He was to taste it again in 1815.

- What happened at Waterloo?
- Why is it considered one of the great battles of all time?

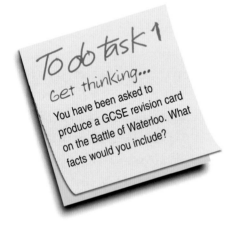

To do task 1
Get thinking...
You have been asked to produce a GCSE revision card on the Battle of Waterloo. What facts would you include?

Napoleon and Wellington would meet for a decisive battle in the countryside south of the Belgium capital, Brussels.

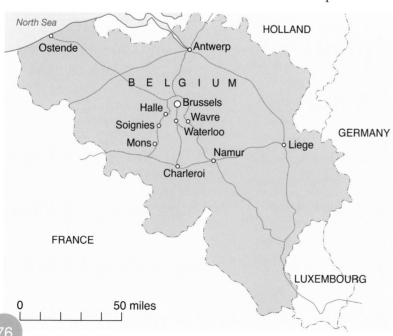

Why was there a battle at Waterloo?

Trafalgar, however, failed to end the conflict between Britain and France, and so the war with Napoleon continued. Both countries blocked important trade routes for the other, causing grain prices to rise quickly in Britain, which in turn led to civil unrest and rioting. The British government countered this by introducing the Corn laws in 1804, which would protect the interests of British farmers.

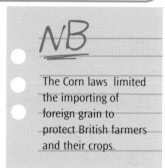

NB

The Corn laws limited the importing of foreign grain to protect British farmers and their crops.

France continued to threaten further aggression in Europe, and Napoleon was only defeated after his failed invasion of Russia in 1812. The vast distances his troops and supplies had to cover, plus the harsh weather and Russian **resistance**, combined to inflict losses on France of 400,000 troops. Defeated, Napoleon was forced to **abdicate**. He was imprisoned on the Mediterranean island of Elba, and France's allies broke their previous allegiances and turned, instead, to support Britain.

A fresh crisis

The French were gradually forced out of their European territories, with the last place to show any resistance being Belgium. Britain's troops therefore established semi-permanent bases there and that is where they were when news reached them that Napoleon had escaped from his prison, in March 1815.

The hero of the British armed forces, Wellington, did not learn of Napoleon's escape immediately, but when he did he was confident that sufficient troops could be raised to tackle the new threat. He thought that he could rely on troops from Britain, Austria, Switzerland, Italy and the Netherlands, among others. Napoleon would be massively outnumbered.

Napoleon knew, however, that if he could defeat Wellington and his army he would have a clear passage through Europe, so he attempted to engage him in battle before reinforcements could arrive to boost Wellington's small army. Wellington could initially only rely on the help of the Prussian army, led by Field Marshall Blücher. It was these two small forces that would defend Belgium and the allies against the new threat from Napoleon.

Wellington

Sir Arthur Wellesley was given the title Lord Wellington in 1809, for services to his country. Born in Ireland, he was an experienced military campaigner, respected by all around him. He had returned to military service to take on the might of Napoleon after a number of years in politics.

The two armies eventually met at Waterloo.

Sir Arthur Wellesley, Lord Wellington, a portrait from an 1860's engraving.

Source A — The Battle of Waterloo, from the BBC website

*"The Battle of Waterloo was fought thirteen kilometres south of Brussels between the French, under the command of Napoleon Bonaparte, and the Allied armies commanded by the Duke of Wellington from Britain and General Blücher from Prussia. The French defeat at Waterloo drew to a close 23 years of war beginning with the French **Revolutionary** wars in 1792 and continuing with the Napoleonic Wars from 1803. There was a brief eleven-month respite when Napoleon was forced to abdicate, exiled to the island of Elba. However, the unpopularity of Louis XVIII and the economic and social instability of France motivated him to return to Paris in March 1815. The Allies soon declared war once again."*

To do task 2
Comprehension
1. Where is Waterloo?
2. Which European army backed up the British?
3. Who led the British forces?

BUZZ WORDZZ

Abdicate
Imperial
Resistance
Revolutionary

The battle

On Sunday 18 June 1815, the Battle of Waterloo began. The British army and Prussian troops were forced to confront Napoleon before their allies from Austria and Russia arrived to help. Napoleon knew that his only chance of winning was to defeat the Allies separately, rather than all together. Napoleon first attacked the Prussians, before they met up with Wellington's British forces. He thought he had defeated them, but the Prussians merely regrouped and later came to reinforce Wellington's army.

When Napoleon's army confronted Wellington's, 180,000 men squashed themselves onto a battlefield 3 miles wide and 1 mile deep. Wellington's troops took shelter from cannon fire behind the Mont St Jean ridge , but were hopelessly pounded by the big guns of Napoleon's forces.

The terrain of the battlefield made fighting difficult. Heavy rain meant that Napoleon's troops were struggling through mud and in places had to make their way through fields of corn. Both factors made it difficult to move the all-important heavy guns into position.

Source C

Waterloo: Napoleon's Last Gamble,

Andrew Roberts, HarperPerennial, 2006

"*Napoleon's plan was to break the enemy's centre, gain possession of the slopes of Mount St Jean and thus split Wellington's army in half while controlling the all important road to Brussels.*"

Source B

Dancing into Battle, *Nick Foulkes, Phoenix, 2007*

"*As far as anyone can tell the battle of Waterloo began at around half past eleven, although estimates vary between 11am and 1:50pm. The sun had risen to reveal the two armies, Wellington's of approximately 73,200 looking south towards a French force of 77,500, each army on a ridge of ground, facing the other across a gently undulating plain covered in the high crops that characterised the Flanders countryside that summer. At times the two forces were separated by little more than a couple of hundred yards.*"

Source D The History of Britain and Ireland,

Mike Corbishley, John Gillingham, Rosemanry Kelly, Ian Dawson, James Mason and Kenneth O. Morgan, Oxford University Press, 2006

"*Survivors faltered, deaf and bruised by the recoil of the muskets. The wounded men were carried on blankets to doctors. There they were gagged, blindfolded and held down while injured limbs were hacked off to prevent death by infection. Legs and arms were piled in heaps.*"

To do task 3

Get thinking...

Imagine that you are one of the soldiers in the picture below. What was the battle like? How did you feel? Use the information in Sources B, C and D to help you describe the events.

The fighting itself was brutal and fierce. The soldiers could not escape the cannon and musket shot that swept across the battlefield.

The French and British forces were fairly evenly matched, but the timely re-appearance of the Prussians, at around 1.00pm, to Wellington's right, drew some French troops away from the main battle and turned the battle in the Allies' favour. Their support bolstered British power and enabled Wellington to bring about a decisive victory.

The shattered French forces were driven from the battlefield. Finally, Napoleon had been defeated, bringing his rule to an end and seeing the restoration of the French monarchy.

Source E

Generals: Ten British Commanders who Shaped the World, Mark Urban, Faber & Faber, 2006

"Judging his moment to perfection, Wellington waited until the leading French were less than 100 yards away before shouting, 'Up Guards! Make ready!' The redcoats stood, cocked their weapons, levelled them and let fly a hideous, crashing volley. Scores of **Imperial** Guardsmen dropped to the ground, the battalions swaying collectively from this terrible shock."

Source F

Waterloo: Napoleon's Last Gamble, Andrew Roberts, HarperPerennial, 2006

"Ghastly as the carnage at Waterloo undoubtedly was, thenceforth wars were to be fought with the infinitely more ghastly methods of trenches (the Crimea), barbed wire, railways and machine guns (the American Civil War), directed starvation (the Franco-Prussian War), concentration camps (the Boer War) and mustard gas and aerial bombardment (the First World War). By the time of the Great War, chivalry was effectively dead as an element of war-making."

To do task 4
Get creative...

Produce a storyboard showing the events of the Battle of Waterloo.

Discussion POINT ?

Should leaders be on the battlefield with the men or in safety behind the lines?

The Crimean War, 1854–56, was a war of innovation and change.

- Why was it a turning point in the history of warfare?
- What lasting effect did it have?

Why was there a war?

The Crimean War was essentially a war between Britain and Russia, fought to try and control trade routes. It was financed in Britain by an increase in income tax, much to the dislike of the British people. Tax was raised from 7d (7 pennies) to 1 shilling (1 shilling = 12 pennies = 5 new pence) in the pound.

Source A

The Rise and Fall of the British Empire,
Lawrence James, Abacus, 1995

"No territory was at stake; the war was undertaken solely to guarantee British naval supremacy in the Mediterranean and, indirectly, to forestall any threat to India which might have followed Russia replacing Britain as the dominant power in the Middle East."

To do task 1

Get reporting...

You have been given the responsibility for writing a report for the government on the state of the British army in the 1850s. Use the information on these pages to produce your report.

Despite the recent history of conflict between Britain and France, at the time of the Crimean War they were allies because they were both concerned about the power of Russia. They wanted to stop Russia expanding its empire into areas of Europe such as the Black Sea, the Balkans and the eastern Mediterranean. In 1853 Russia had declared war on Turkey, prompted by arguments about the Holy Land. This fuelled fears that Russia intended to take advantage of the decaying Turkish Empire, and drew Britain and France further into the conflict.

The armies

In the 1850s, Britain's army was ill-equipped and poorly led. After the triumph of Waterloo it had been neglected financially by the government for many years. Although it was the army of a huge imperial power, it had little practice fighting against effective forces. Even the traditional bright red uniforms (seen in the illustration on the left) worn by its soldiers were outdated and unsuitable for most battlefields.

Morale was low during the Crimean War and the conditions soldiers lived and fought in led to casualties from numerous diseases, particularly cholera, malaria and dysentery. Despite these difficulties, the courage of the regular soldier was generally without question. Unfortunately the soldiers were let down by their commanders, who were quite simply out of their depth.

Lord Raglan was in charge of the British army during the Crimean War but, as Source B shows, he was typical of the age and experience of most British army commanders.

Many of key leaders in the British army were elderly and not used to modern battle techniques. Quite simply, weapons, tactics and ideas about warfare had moved on considerably since the Napoleonic Wars 40 years previously. And some British generals had not. To the horror of their French allies, many British generals regarded the Crimea more like an adventure holiday than a war zone.

To do task 2
Comprehension
1. Why did the Crimean War begin?
2. What problems affected British troops?
3. Who was Lord Raglan?

Source B Someone has Blundered, *Denis Judd, Weidenfeld and Nicolson, 1999*

"He was sixty-six years of age when Britain entered the Crimean War, and had seen no action since the Napoleonic Wars. On the field of Waterloo his right elbow had been shattered by a musket-ball, and he had let the surgeon amputate his damaged arm between the shoulder and the elbow without a murmur. As the surgeon tossed the arm away, Raglan called out 'Hey, bring my arm back. There's a ring my wife gave me on the finger.'"

Source C

Someone has Blundered,
Denis Judd, Weidenfeld and Nicolson, 1999

"To many French officers the British looked absurdly amateurish, and at least fifty years behind the times. Many officers brought their favourite horses, as if to hunt foxes; they also brought servants and tweed suits. Several brought their wives along too. The personal luggage of the British officers astounded the French, and it was noticed that the Duke of Cambridge's baggage filled seventeen carts."

PRINCE MENSCHIKOFF, LATE COMMANDER OF THE RUSSIAN FORCES IN THE CRIMEA.

The leader of the Russian forces in the Crimea was Prince Menschikov.

NB
Prince Aleksandr Sergeyevich Menschikov was in charge of both the Russian army and naval forces.

Fortunately for the English, the Russian army they were facing was also poorly led and even worse equipped. The Russians were led by Prince Aleksandr Sergeyevich Menschikov.

To do task 3

Get thinking...

Look at the list of innovations (on the right) that came out of the Crimean war. Which was the most important and why?

Despite the lack of preparation and the inexperience of some of the military leaders, the Crimean War has become characterised by some real **innovation** such as:

- the use of **telegrams** for communication
- the use of railways for the transport of troops and supplies
- the use of explosive shells in artillery, for the first time
- the French Minie rifle was used (later modified to produce the British Lee Enfield rifle) instead of the previous musket
- the setting up of the International Red Cross charity.

All these innovations transformed the way that future wars would be fought.

The battles

The Allied armies, numbering 60,000 in total, landed in the Crimea at Kalamatia Bay on 14 September 1854. Kalamatia is just north of Sevastopol, a Russian naval base on the Crimean peninsular. After their landing in the Crimea, a number of battles and confrontations with the Russians followed.

Map of the Crimea, showing the location of the main battles.

Battle of Alma River, September 1854: A British and French victory. Russian troops and their commanders were under-prepared and complacent.

Battle of Balaklava, October 1854: Famous in history as the scene of the Charge of the Light Brigade, in which orders were misunderstood, leading to the unnecessary death of hundreds of British cavalrymen.

Battle of Inkerman, November 1854: Despite poor weather, which reduced the battle to a series of hand-to-hand combats, it was a British and French victory. Russian casualties were approximately 12,000 killed and wounded.

Source D — Siege of Sevastapol September 1855,

from the National Maritime Museum website

"The strong and heavily fortified Black Sea port of Sevastopol, on the south-west coast of the Crimea, was the main naval base of the Russian Black Sea Fleet. During the Crimean War (1853–56), the capture or destruction of this stronghold became the main military object of the allied British, French and Turkish armies opposing Russia. Sevastopol endured an 11-month siege before finally capitulating to the enemy in September 1855."

The Crimean War ended in the spring of 1856, with the Russians accepting defeat. Despite the victory, the Crimean War had been a humiliating experience for the British because it exposed the incompetence of its leaders, the desperate conditions suffered by the British soldiers, and the poor standards of equipment and tactical thinking within the British army.

Reporting the war

You may be surprised to learn that the Crimean War was the first conflict in which newspaper reports were sent back to Britain. This allowed information from the war zone to be shared with the general population. Although there was a delay of several weeks between the battles taking place and the reports appearing in the British press, this was still a huge **innovation** in the way everyday people at home got their views of events abroad.

The main voice behind the reporting was W.H. Russell, a war correspondent for *The Times*. Reporting also illustrated the war through photographers, such as Roger Fenton, who took captivating images that revealed the true horrors of war, and artists such as William Simpson.

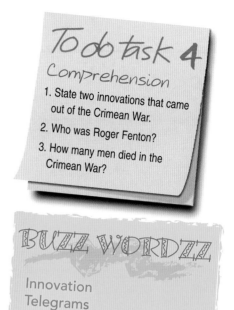

To do task 4
Comprehension
1. State two innovations that came out of the Crimean War.
2. Who was Roger Fenton?
3. How many men died in the Crimean War?

BUZZ WORDZZ

Innovation
Telegrams

An original photograph of troops from the Crimean War, by Roger Fenton (left) and William Simpson's painting of a mortar battery bombarding the besieged city of Sebastopol, during the Crimean War (right).

Source E

A Brief History of The Crimean War,
Alexis Troubetzkoy, Robinson, 2006

"From the declaration of war to the signing of the peace, 28 months passed. During that period over half a million men died. In all theatres, it is estimated that the allies lost 252,000 men, and the Russians 246,000. They died on the battlefields, in hospitals, at sea and on the steppes. They died by bullet and by shrapnel, of cholera and disease, of starvation and of the freezing cold. In Sevastopol alone over 102,000 defenders were killed, wounded or reported missing."

Discussion POINT

Does publicity help or hinder warfare?

Florence Nightingale and Mary Seacole played a major role in the Crimean War, transforming the way that soldiers were cared for.

- Who were they?
- What did they do in the Crimean War?
- Why are they famous?

To do task 1

Comprehension

1. When was Florence Nightingale born?

2. What was the hospital called that she worked in?

3. What was Mary Seacole's nickname?

BUZZ WORDZZ

Appalling

A tale of two nurses

The Crimean War is remembered more for two nurses than for the actual fighting. Florence Nightingale and Mary Seacole are often remembered as nurses, but they were also good administrators, managers and innovators. They helped to change the way that the soldiers were cared for and set a pattern for future reforms in hospitals and nursing.

Florence Nightingale

Florence Nightingale was born in 1820 to a wealthy family and trained as a nurse in Germany. On her return to England she worked in a hospital in Harley Street, London. When reports came from the Crimea about the appalling conditions the soldiers endured, Nightingale was asked by the Secretary of State for War to go to the Crimea, taking 38 nurses with her.

Nightingale's war work began at Scutari Military Hospital. As in most military hospitals at this time, the soldiers had a bigger chance of dying from disease such as cholera than from their wounds. Hospital hygiene was **appalling** and poor drainage and sewage systems made the situation worse. Nightingale realised that she would have to tackle more than just the hospital wards. So she set about sorting out the laundry supplies, the kitchens, sanitation and food preparation facilities.

Nightingale did improve conditions hugely. After the war she went on to establish disciplined training for nurses and efficient hospital planning all over Britain. She helped to make nursing a highly regarded profession for women.

Nightingale and her work are commemorated on the Crimean War Memorial in Pall Mall, London.

Mary Seacole

Mary Seacole was born in 1805, in Jamaica. Her mother was Jamaican and her father was Scottish. He had come to the Caribbean as a soldier, where he had met Seacole's mother. Mary, therefore, had an affinity to both Britain and her home country of Jamaica, especially as Jamaica was part of the British Empire at this time. Mary gained medical experience by looking after wounded soldiers who were stationed in the Caribbean to protect British interests and possessions. When news of the Crimean War reached Mary, she felt that her skills would be valuable in the war zone and, having offered her services to the British, who turned her down, she made her way to the Crimea at her own expense.

Source A **A Brief History of The Crimean War,**

Alexis Troubetzkoy, Robinson, 2006

"She rapidly became a familiar figure to the fighting men, easily identifiable by her outrageously colourful garb and by the mule she led, laden with provisions, bandages and an array of medical equipment. When Sevastopol fell in September 1855, she was the first woman to enter the city, where she passed out refreshments and tended the wounded. Although she became a popular figure with the British public, the Government took a long time to formally recognise her heroism – the Crimean medal was awarded her with little fanfare only years after the war. A black heroine from the Caribbean."

On arrival in the Crimea, Seacole built the 'British Hospital' as close to the battlefields as she could, so that she could provide the best possible service to the soldiers. As well as offering medical care, Seacole also sold provisions and food. Nightingale once described the hospital as little more than a 'brothel', but this only showed the rivalry between the two women.

Although rejected by the British establishment, Seacole contributed enormously to the well-being of the soldiers, earning herself the nickname 'Mother Seacole'. By the time she left the Crimea, she had spent a huge amount of her own money on improving the conditions for many British soldiers.

On her return to England, Seacole wrote a book about her life, *Wonderful Adventures of Mrs Seacole*, which became a best-seller at the time.

The front cover to Mary Seacole's book, published in 1857.

To do task 2
Get creative...
Using the information on pages 84 and 85, write an obituary for either Florence Nightingale or Mary Seacole.

To do task 3
Get thinking...
You have to decide who to build a statue in remembrance of: Mary Seacole or Florence Nightingale. Who would you choose and why?

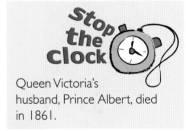

Stop the Clock
Queen Victoria's husband, Prince Albert, died in 1861.

Introduction

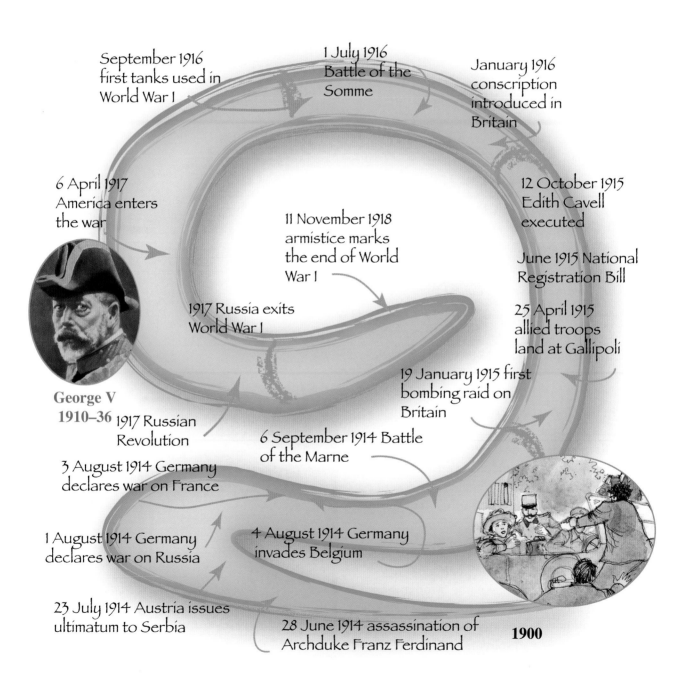

September 1916 first tanks used in World War I

1 July 1916 Battle of the Somme

January 1916 conscription introduced in Britain

6 April 1917 America enters the war

11 November 1918 armistice marks the end of World War I

12 October 1915 Edith Cavell executed

June 1915 National Registration Bill

25 April 1915 allied troops land at Gallipoli

1917 Russia exits World War I

George V 1910–36 1917 Russian Revolution

19 January 1915 first bombing raid on Britain

6 September 1914 Battle of the Marne

3 August 1914 Germany declares war on France

1 August 1914 Germany declares war on Russia

4 August 1914 Germany invades Belgium

23 July 1914 Austria issues ultimatum to Serbia

28 June 1914 assassination of Archduke Franz Ferdinand

1900

One shot!

When three shots were fired by 19-year-old Gavrilo Princip, on 28 June 1914, few people suspected it would lead to war. Princip – a Serbian revolutionary – **assassinated** Archduke Franz Ferdinand and his wife in their open-top car during their visit to Sarajevo. Ferdinand was the heir to the Austro-Hungarian throne, but his murder set off a chain of events that led to the outbreak of World War I, also known as the Great War.

Austrians saw the shooting of the Archduke as an act of terrorism and their ally, Germany, backed them in their desire for revenge. Because of alliances and treaties, a complicated chain of events then unfolded.

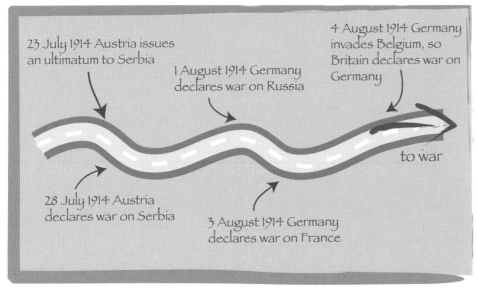

23 July 1914 Austria issues an ultimatum to Serbia

1 August 1914 Germany declares war on Russia

4 August 1914 Germany invades Belgium, so Britain declares war on Germany

to war

28 July 1914 Austria declares war on Serbia

3 August 1914 Germany declares war on France

But why did all these nations become involved so quickly?

The Great War of 1914–18 will never be forgotten. Nearly 8 million people lost their lives during this conflict and over 20 million were wounded. It was truly a 'World War'.

- How did it start?
- Who was to blame?

Source A

Forgotten Voices of the Great War,
Max Arthur, Ebury Press, 2004

"In the glorious sunshine of June 1914 there was no thought of war, no international crisis and no hint that the crowned heads of Europe were poised to tumble one after the other. The assassination of the heir to the Austro-Hungarian Empire by a Serb sponsored terrorist on 28th June was neither predictable nor inevitable. Yet within weeks, millions of men were on the march. On 4th August with Austria and Germany already at war with Russia and France, and with German troops marching into Belgium on their way to Paris, Britain declared war on Germany."

To do task 1
Comprehension
1. Whose shooting sparked off World War I?
2. Who was Britain allied with at the start of the war?
3. What was the main aim of the Schlieffen Plan?

NB

The Schlieffen Plan was so complicated that it had taken over nine years to finalise the finer points. Although it formed the basis of most German military planning at the time, it was modified in 1906, leaving a reduced force to attack France from the north.

The alliances

In 1914 two major power alliances existed in Europe. These were:

- the Triple Alliance: Germany, Austria-Hungary and Italy

- the Triple Entente: France, Russia and Britain

They had all agreed to protect and assist each other if any country was aggressive towards, or threatened their allies. The alliances had formed because all these nations were rivals for land for their empires, trade for their goods and for political power. The alliances were designed to protect these interests against their rivals. Britain, initially, remained neutral until German armies entered Belgium on their way to attack France as part of the 'Schlieffen Plan' (see Source B).

The Schlieffen Plan

The German minister of war, von Schlieffen, had drawn up a plan in 1905 to avoid having to fight a war on two fronts: with both France and Russia at the same time. The plan relied on defeating France quickly and assuming that Russia would be slow in mobilising her troops. It also assumed that Britain would not get involved. By contrast, it depended on the German forcess moving very quickly indeed. The plan was for Germany to swing forces through neutral countries and attack France from the north, then swiftly defeat the French armies. After this Germany would rapidly move its troops by rail to take on Russia.

The plan proved over-ambitious. In reality, Russia mobilised her troops quickly and Germany found far more resistance in Belgium than anticipated.

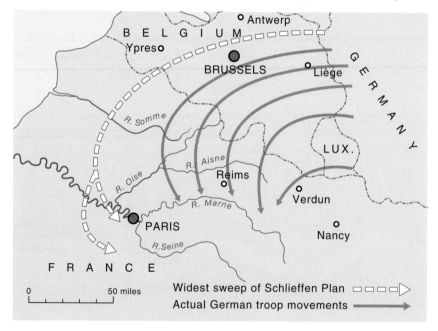

Source B

The First World War in Photographs,
Richard Holmes, Bookmart, 2007

"Germany's violation of Belgian neutrality, which had been guaranteed by a treaty to which Britain was a signatory, made it difficult for her to stand aside. In any event the Foreign Secretary, Sir Edward Grey, pointed out that a German victory would be bad for British interests, and, when Germany declined to withdraw from Belgium, Britain declared war on her on August 4th."

Britain enters the war

On 4 August 1914 Britain declared war on Germany, after German forces had ignored the fact that Belgium was a neutral country and insisted on passing over Belgian territory to attack France.

The first truly 'world' war had begun.

Why were new recruits needed?

Waging war meant more than just words, it meant action. In 1914, Britain had only a small army because it relied mainly on its navy for protection. Part of the army was a specially trained mobile unit of 120,000 men, known as the British Expeditionary Force (BEF). Led by Sir John French, this force had been trained to travel anywhere in the world, to defend Britain's empire.

Kitchener's call to action inspired many to volunteer for armed service.

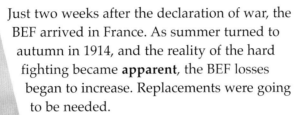

Just two weeks after the declaration of war, the BEF arrived in France. As summer turned to autumn in 1914, and the reality of the hard fighting became **apparent**, the BEF losses began to increase. Replacements were going to be needed.

As in Germany and France, the call for volunteers in Britain was met with huge enthusiasm. Lord Kitchener, Secretary of State for War, thought that 100,000 men would join up, but he ended up with nearly 2.5 million volunteers by the end of 1915.

Joining up

Many men who joined up expected the war to be over by Christmas, which meant that it would not be a long-term commitment. It seemed an exciting opportunity for adventure, and to get away from home and work. Government **recruitment** posters encouraged men to join up. They also spread **propaganda** about German atrocities (horrific behaviour) inflicted on civilians, to whip up anti-German feeling and persuade more men to volunteer (see Source A).

When war broke out, the British government needed soldiers to fight.

- How did they persuade people to join up?
- Who fought for Britain?

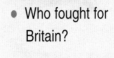

To do task 1

Get creative...

It is your job to design a poster to encourage men to join the army. Look at the posters shown on this page. What would you include and what message would you send?

How does this British propaganda poster depict the German enemy?

Source A

Forgotten Voices of the Great War,
Max Arthur, Ebury Press, 2004

Sergeant Stefan Westmann – 29th Division, German Army

"In one small village the mayor came and asked our company commander not to allow us to cut off the hands of children. These were atrocity stories that we heard about the German army. At first we laughed about it, but when we heard of other propaganda things they said against the German army, we became angry."

The government also boosted enthusiasm for the war by showing rousing war films designed to increase **patriotism** (see Source B).

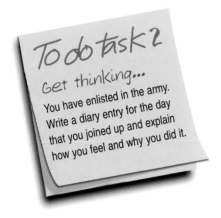

To do task 2

Get thinking...

You have enlisted in the army. Write a diary entry for the day that you joined up and explain how you feel and why you did it.

Source B

Forgotten Voices of the Great War,
Max Arthur, Ebury Press, 2004

Private William Dove – 16th Lancers

"War had been declared, and the following Sunday I went with a friend of mine to Shepherd's Bush Empire to see the film show. At the end they showed the fleet sailing the high seas and played 'Britons Never Shall be Slaves' and 'Hearts of Oak'. And you know, one feels that little shiver run up the back and you know you have got to do something. I had just turned seventeen at that time and on the Monday I went up to Whitehall – Old Scotland Yard – and enlisted in the 16th Lancers."

A scene repeated thousands of times across Europe in 1914: a soldier says goodbye to his loved one.

During the four years of war that followed, over 65 million men from more than 30 countries were called up. Men joined up with great enthusiasm on all sides. New soldiers were marched off in street parades, where flowers were thrown at the new recruits and they were given cigarettes and chocolates. Joining up was celebrated in public, with wives and children often accompanying their menfolk through the streets. The governments continued to feed propaganda through posters, films and the media, to hype up patriotic fervour and blacken the public perception of the 'enemy'.

The physical requirements
Initially recruits had to:

- be between 18 and 30 years old
- be at least 5ft 6in tall
- have a chest that measured at least 34ins.

However, these requirements were not stuck to rigidly. Some boys as young as 13 joined up, because birth certificates were rarely inspected and recruiting officers relied on their own judgement as to whether candidates were mature enough. Minimum height restrictions were relaxed in some places, to enable more men to join up.

Pals Battalions

One of the reasons why initial recruitment was so successful was the popularity of the 'Pals' or 'Chums' **Battalions**. The idea of these battalions was to persuade men to join up with their friends and work colleagues, so they could serve together.

These are some of the battalions that were formed:

- Tyneside Irish
- Footballers' Battalion
- Stockbrokers' Battalion
- Glasgow Tramways' Battalion
- Post Office Rifles
- Accrington Pals

- Judeans – Jewish volunteers
- Leeds Pals
- Public Schools' Battalion
- Grimsby Chums
- Hull Commercials

However, a terrible disadvantage of the Pals Battalions scheme was that, as well as training together, men also fought and often died together. Deliberately kept alongside each other as a unit, the Pals Battalions were sent into attack together as well. There was a terrible risk that many men would be killed or injured. If coming from the same community, it meant that whole villages and towns lost large proportions of their young men. For example, during the Battle of the Somme in 1916, 750 of the 900 Leeds Pals were killed, and 584 of the 720 Accrington Pals.

The trauma of small communities losing often hundreds of sons, husbands, brothers and fathers more or less at the same time, was a terrible feature of the Great War.

NB

Although Pals Battalions had first been suggested by General Henry Rawlinson, the first example of a Pals Battalion was set up in Liverpool by a man called Lord Derby.

Many of the Accrington Pals did not return home to their loved ones.

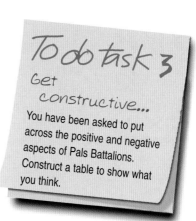

BUZZ WORDZZ

Apparent
Assassinated
Battalion
Patriotism
Propaganda
Recruitment

To do task 3
Get constructive...
You have been asked to put across the positive and negative aspects of Pals Battalions. Construct a table to show what you think.

Women encouraged men to join up, often handing them the sign of cowardice: a white feather.

Source C

Call-to-Arms,

Charles Messenger,
Cassell, 2006

"Our first instructions were to let everything go rusty. Nothing was to be polished – buttons, cap badges, buckles, stirrup irons – anything that could reflect sunlight and so give notice of our presence in France."

Billeted
Billeted meant that soldiers were often forced upon householders who had spare rooms, or were assigned quarters in unoccupied houses.

Soldiers were taught to hate their enemy and to be ready for hand-to-hand combat. Here they practise with their rifle bayonet – a short dagger that could be attached to the end of the rifle.

The White Feather Campaign

Some women played their part in encouraging men to join up. The White Feather Campaign was set up to humiliate men into joining. The women patrolled streets and town centres, handing out white feathers (a symbol of cowardice) to men who appeared to be eligible to join up but who were not in uniform.

Conscription

As 1914 gave way to 1915, thousands of men were killed and had to be replaced. Volunteer numbers fell as the truth about the war in France emerged. It was now obviously not going to be a quick victory, and the fighting men's conditions were appalling. The government increased the maximum age for recruitment and in June 1915 introduced the National Registration Bill for men and women aged 15–65. This meant that everybody had to register their details, showing whether or not they were available to fight in the war. This showed that there were 3.4 million men in Britain who were eligible for war but had not volunteered.

To take advantage of these extra men the government brought in conscription in January 1916, which meant they could call up any single men aged between 18 and 41 to join the army. In May, this was extended to married men as well. The only men excluded from this were those unfit for service or doing important jobs for the war effort. By April 1918, an extra 2.5 million soldiers had been found through conscription.

Training

Although the 'new armies', as these new recruits were known, could not hope to reach the level of training and expertise that regular professional BEF soldiers had, all soldiers went through an intensive period of basic training, often concluding in France's infamous 'Bull Ring' based at Étaples. During this period of training they were taught what to expect in the trenches, how to fight in battle (see Source C) and how to hate the enemy .

New troops would be billeted with families either in England or France while undergoing their training.

Empire troops

During the Great War, Britain still had a large empire that reached across the globe, including: India, Australia, New Zealand, the Caribbean and parts of Africa. Although the inhabitants of these countries were not British, they still joined the fight for Britain and her allies.

Soldiers from Australia and New Zealand

The ANZACs (Australian and New Zealand Army Corps) were formed from excellent soldiers and were gladly received by the British. Australia offered 30,000 troops to the war effort in August 1914 (see Source D).

ANZAC soldiers seen on their way to attack Turkish forces at Gallipoli.

Source D

The Rise and Fall of the British Empire,

Lawrence James, Abacus, 1995

"The banners of England unfurled across the sea,
Floating out upon the wind, were beckoning to me
Storm rent and battle-torn, smoke stained and grey:
The banners of England – and how could I stay!"

Australia also tried on two occasions to introduce conscription but it was twice voted against – 1916 and 1917.

Soldiers from India

Many Indian men were willing to join in the war effort, particularly at the start when it was widely believed that it would be a short war. In total more than 1.4 million Indian citizens fought for Britain and her allies. Some served in the Royal Flying Corps as well as the Army.

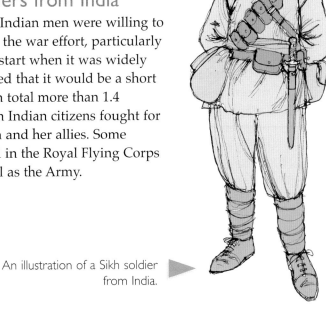

An illustration of a Sikh soldier from India.

Discussion POINT ?

What is British?

To do task 4
Comprehension

1. What was conscription?
2. What was the White Feather Campaign?
3. Why were soldiers from the British Empire important to the British war effort?

An illustration of a soldier from the Caribbean.

Soldiers from the Caribbean

West Indian soldiers saw action on many battle fronts, most notably the Middle East, France and Italy. Some were pilots in the newly formed Royal Flying Corps.

Racism in the armies

Despite outstanding bravery and a high level of performance, some soldiers of the Empire suffered racial slights and abuse. Black soldiers were often relegated to menial tasks. Soldiers from South Africa left behind a racist climate only to find a similar one when they reached the war zones. The British West Indies Regiment (BWIR) was subjected to such racist abuse that the soldiers mutinied in 1918 (see Source E).

Caibbean troops stockpiling artillery shells.

Stop the clock

Japan entered the Great War on 23 August 1914.

To do task 5

Get creative...

Produce a guide to the recruitment of 'British' soldiers in the Great War. Include all the different races from the Empire plus the basic recruitment information.

Discussion POINT ?

Why do you think that soldiers from the British Empire were subjected to racism, despite fighting on the same side as those handing out the insults?

Source E

From the history pages of the BBC website

"After Armistice Day, on 11 November 1918, the eight BWIR battalions in France and Italy were concentrated at Taranto in Italy to prepare for demobilisation. They were subsequently joined by the three battalions from Egypt and the men from Mesopotamia. As a result of severe labour shortages at Taranto, the West Indians had to assist with loading and unloading ships and do labour fatigues. This led to much resentment, and on 6 December 1918 the men of the 9th Battalion revolted and attacked their officers. On the same day, 180 sergeants forwarded a petition to the Secretary of State complaining about the pay issue, the failure to increase their separation allowance, and the fact that they had been discriminated against in the area of promotions."

Should I or shouldn't I?

The introduction of **conscription** meant that there was huge pressure on men to join up. As more men joined the army, either voluntarily or by conscription, women took over many of the jobs that the men left vacant, including working in **munitions** factories and driving buses.

Some men, however, chose not to fight. These men were called **conscientious** objectors or 'conshies' and there were about 20,000 in all. As the name suggests, it was often a case of their consciences not allowing them to fight. Either they were pacifists who believed in peace, such as the Quakers, or they simply objected to others removing their free-will and telling them that they had to go to war.

Not all conscientious objectors chose not to go to war: they simply chose not to fight. Some of these men took on non-fighting roles in the army, such as ambulance drivers, cooks, medical assistants or stretcher-bearers. They worked on the front lines alongside the troops.

Other men decided to help the war effort but didn't join the army. They took on civilian roles and were called alternativists.

A relatively small number of men (about 1,000) refused to contribute at all to the war effort. They believed the war was wrong and they were called absolutists.

Tribunals

All conscientious objectors (COs) had to face **tribunals** (interview panels with a legal authority) that would look at each case to check that the men had genuine moral objections to joining up. These tribunals were run by local councils and often included older businessmen, shopkeepers, landowners and retired military men (like those illustrated on the right). There was always one military representative present, whose main aim was to recruit as many men as possible for the army.

The COs did not always get a sympathetic hearing from tribunals, and relatively few were granted full exemption from joining up. Those who refused to join up could be sent to prison, and almost 6,000 men were.

Consequences

COs who ended up in prison were often treated very harshly. Over 70 died while in prison, as a result of illness or depression, and many more suffered long-term physical or mental illness.

Some people refused to fight in the Great War.

- Why did people decide not to fight?
- What happened to them?

BUZZ WORDZZ

Conscientious
Conscription
Munitions
Tribunals

The only support for the COs came from a handful of MPs and peace groups, the most prominent of which was the No-Conscription Fellowship (NCF). The NCF gave moral support and some practical help to COs and their families. It also campaigned against the harsh treatment suffered by imprisoned COs.

The Home Guard platoon made famous in 'Dad's Army'.

After the end of the war in November 1918, there was a delay in releasing many of the COs from prison. Some remained there for another six months. Even on release, they faced difficulties. Many people refused to employ them and signs such as 'COs and absolutists need not apply' appeared in job adverts.

The following is an extract from the 1970s TV series 'Dad's Army', a comedy set in World War II. One of the elderly members of the Home Guard, Godfrey, reveals that he was a conscientious objector in World War I and he suffers prejudice because of these actions, as many men did.

To do task 1

Get thinking...

You have to make the decision whether or not to fight for your country. Make a list of all the 'for' and 'against' factors to help you decide.

Discussion POINT ?

People should have a conscience where war is concerned.

Godfrey: Don't you understand, sir — if I couldn't bring myself to kill that mouse — how could I ever kill a German?

Mainwaring: But if you felt like that, why did you join the Home Guard in the first place?

Godfrey: Well, when the Home Guard was first started, things were so desperate — I somehow felt different from last time.

Mainwaring: Things are still desperate, Godfrey — Hitler could invade at any moment. And we need every man we can get. But what did you mean when you said you felt different from the last time?

Godfrey: Well you see, sir — during the last war I was a conscientious objector.

Mainwaring: What?

Godfrey: A conscientious objector.

Mainwaring (half rising): A con … (He can't even bring himself to say the word — his voice goes cold) You mean you didn't want to fight?

Godfrey: No, not really, sir.

Mainwaring: I can't believe it, Godfrey, I really can't. (Pause) I think the best thing you can do at the moment is to go home.

'Dad's Army', Series 3, Episode 11 © BBC 1969
Originally performed by: Arnold Ridley as Private Godfrey; Arthur Lowe as Captain Mainwaring; John Le Mesurier as Sergeant Wilson.

The trench systems

The opposing armies dug themselves into trenches: the Germans on one side, the British and French on the other. The next four years was a slow 'war of attrition', with each side launching attacks to break through enemy lines, and at the same time wearing each other down (see Source A).

Source A **Trench Warfare, 1914–18,** Tony Ashworth, Pan Books, 2004

"During 1915 and 1916 the position of the Allied armies was relatively static. On the northernmost point of the Western Front, the Belgian army held a sector approximately 15 miles long from Nieuport to a point just north of the Ypres Salient. The British and Commonwealth armies were entrenched along 85 miles from the Ypres Salient to the River Somme, and between the Somme and Switzerland lay the French army."

Trench warfare is one of the most notorious features of World War I.

- **What were the trenches?**
- **What was life like in the trenches?**

A map showing the extent of the trench system on the Western Front.

The trenches ran for a huge length across Europe from the North Sea to Switzerland. Such an expanse of trench systems inevitably meant a huge variety of conditions. The popular image you might have already of trenches being mud, rats, endless puddles and misery may have been true in certain parts of the line but not in all.

Different types of trench

There was a large difference in the quality of trenches between the countries. The Germans had excellent trench systems, much better and deeper than many others. Generally, German trench systems were situated on the best tactical ground in an area, were well made and provided a reasonable standard of comfort for officers and men. Essentially this was because the German generals realised quite quickly that the war of movement had passed, and stalemate or static warfare was now the plan. Therefore they had every intention of staying put in their trenches for a long time.

By contrast, the British forces took a long time to realise and accept this, and as a result their trenches were believed to be only temporary and not as well built or equipped. Only over the course of the war did this approach change. By contrast again, the French often had very shallow trenches.

Trench systems were not simply long straight lines. Parallel lines of front and reserve trenches, with connecting communication trenches between them, snaked their way along valleys, up and over ridges and hills. Where possible they took on a zig-zag pattern. Individual trenches were named and included series of fire-bays and traverses that were designed to stop enemy troops firing down the whole length of the trench, and prevent shell blasts devastating whole lines of exposed trench.

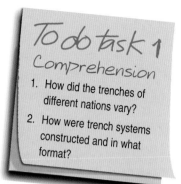

This preserved German trench near Verdun shows the construction of a typical trench and the barbed wire defences that often surrounded them.

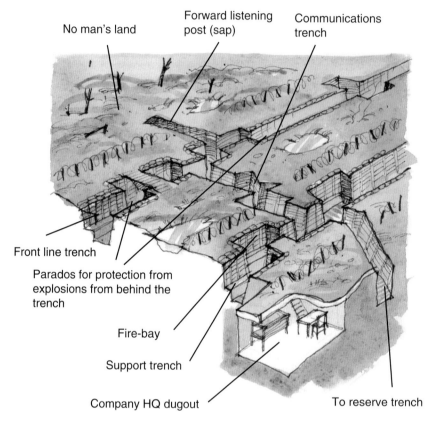

No man's land

Forward listening post (sap)

Communications trench

Front line trench

Parados for protection from explosions from behind the trench

Fire-bay

Support trench

Company HQ dugout

To reserve trench

Communication

To communicate properly the lines of trenches had to be kitted out with appropriate communications. As well as messages sent by runners, communication was mainly by field telephone, so cables had to be laid within and between the trenches.

Once the trench was established, communication was often by telephone.

Life in the trenches

Source B — The Great War,
Correli Barnett, BBC Books, 2003

"While a complex telephone network admirably suited the needs of the static front and the base areas in the rear, it was inadequate as a means of communication and control during an offensive because shellfire again and again cut the lines run out across no-man's land behind the advance. Morse-code wireless sets, heavy and cumbersome, provided only a limited answer. Only with the coming of walkie-talkies in the Second World War would commanders once more enjoy direct contact with their fighting units, as did Marlborough and Wellington. Again and again on the Western Front attacking troops passed out of their commanders' control beyond a gulf of silence or misinformation."

To do task 3

Get thinking...

Write a short story about a soldier's life in the trenches. Use the information in this chapter to help you with the details.

Source C

The Great War, *Correli Barnett, BBC Books, 2003*

"Even on quiet sectors of the front, men lived daily with death and mutilation from the sniper's bullet, the routine salvo of shells, the machine gun fire ripping across no-man's land. Otherwise life on the western front was a matter of tedious routine, of fatigues and discomfort. Middle class war writers were later to paint a dismal picture of the existence in the trenches: the rats in the stinking dug-outs, the hole latrines, the lice in the sweat-stale clothing, the squalid ruination of the whole trench zone. All of it offered a painful enough contrast to the sheltered and comfortable existence enjoyed by these writers before the war. Yet to the majority of soldiers, being peasants or farm labourers or industrial workers from city slums, actual living conditions in and behind the lines on quiet sectors were little if any worse than in peacetime. Certainly many British working-class soldiers enjoyed a better diet, better medical care and better welfare than they had as civilians."

Routine

Troops were rotated through the front-line trenches, spending their remaining time in reserve. Life in the trenches was on the whole boring. Aside from pre-planned 'trench raids', where small groups of men crept out to check enemy positions or capture prisoners for intelligence purposes, the only real activity that the troops got each day was often the 'stand to' every morning, when soldiers manned the fire-step of the trench and were on alert in case of an enemy attack. The rest of the time soldiers were occupied with repairs to trenches, bringing up supplies, or with the continual battle to stay warm, dry and fed.

Source D — From The Long, Long Trail website

"A general pattern for trench routine was 4 days in the front line, then 4 days in close reserve and finally 4 at rest, although this varied enormously depending on conditions, the weather and the availability of enough reserve troops to be able to rotate them in this way. In close reserve, men had to be ready to reinforce the line at very short notice."

Stop the clock

The first poison gas attack came on the 31 January 1915 against Russian troops.

To do task 4
What was the worst part of trench life? Remember that this is only your opinion, but it should be backed by evidence.

Discussion POINT?

How important is it that soldiers get good food?

BUZZ WORDZZ

Latrine

Lice

The water supply was limited, so washing facilities were poor. Most soldiers wore the same clothes for days or weeks at a time and therefore became riddled with lice. These tiny blood suckers were no bigger than a grain of rice and caused intense itching.

Trench foot

Soldiers sometimes suffered this condition, which was a bit like getting frost-bite on their feet. It was caused by having to stand in soaking wet boots often for hours or days at a time. The only cure was to encourage soldiers to avoid it by changing their socks as often as they could (when supplies allowed), and making sure regular inspections of feet were carried out. One idea of rubbing whale grease into their feet in the hope that it would keep out the wet actually turned out to make things even worse!

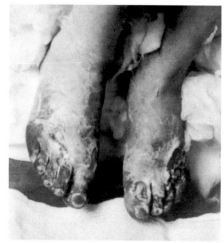

How would you feel about walking if you were suffering with trench foot, like the soldier above is?

Latrines

Toilets in the trenches were known as **latrines** and they definitely weren't private (see Source E).

Source E **The Unknown Soldier: The Story of the Great War,** *Neil Hanson, Corgi, 2007*

"The latrine arrangements were pretty primitive ... the army set aside an area of grass field at the edge of the village where the pioneer or sanitary men dug a dozen little trenches, three feet long by one foot wide and about three feet deep, and without any canvas sacking or anything to hide the view, one dropped one's trousers, bestrode a trench, crouched and attended to nature."

Food

Food was particularly hard to stomach. The main food on offer was bread, 'Bully' beef (corned beef) and Maconochie, which was a meat and vegetable stew in a tin. Soldiers drank water and a daily rum ration. Water was often far from fresh (see Source F).

Soldiers learned how to make different meals from 'Bully' beef. ▶

Source F

The Last Fighting Tommy,
Harry Patch and Richard van Emden, Bloomsbury, 2008

"Despite all the rain, there was little fresh water in the front line as everything we needed had to be carried up. Ration parties would bring the water up in petrol cans which were rarely washed out. ... Washing was almost impossible. Behind the support lines, if you were lucky, you might find an old shell hole where the mud had gradually settled, and the top of the water being reasonably clear, you could get a wash in that."

The fighting

The worst conditions facing the soldiers were during actual trench attacks and battles. Shells of all sizes whistled overhead and machine-gun bullets pinged off the trench walls. The strong smell of cordite wafted across the battlefield as shells and mortars exploded. Some men managed to conquer their fears better than others during these attacks but for, all of them, violent and sudden death was never far away. Living and fighting amid the smell of death and decay was made even worse by a noxious mixture of gas, sweat and excrement.

 A painting showing soldiers going 'over the top'.

Going over the top

The most common form of attack was when large numbers of soldiers climbed out of their trenches, tried to cross the open land ahead and capture the enemy's trenches. This was called 'going over the top' and was, for many, one of the most terrifying part of trench warfare. No Man's Land, the area lying between the trench lines, was usually filled with barbed wire, shell holes, mud, parts of bodies and rusting bits of army equipment. Anyone crossing it was exposed to enemy fire and their chances of survival were slim.

Source G

The Last Tommy Gallery,
from the BBC website

"I always said a prayer before going over the top. .... I'll never forget it. 'Dear God, I am going into grave danger. Please help me to act like a man and come back safe.' And that's what I did. And I went over without fear. That little prayer seemed to save my life because I had no fear left, although there were shells and bullets and all the rest flying when we went over and I were never frightened of being hit. ... And that's true. And six times I went up and six times I said that little prayer and each time I went up and come back safe. And I thank God for it every time."

The popular impression of frontline trenches and the grim, muddy landscape over which soldiers fought and died. Very heavy shelling destroyed the ground and removed all traces of trees or buildings.

Discussion POINT ?

How difficult is it for a soldier to kill?

Source I

Birdsong, *Sebastian Faulks*, Vintage, 1994

"It would make no difference to the outcome of the war whether he himself lived or died; it made no difference whether today it was Turner whose head was blown from his body, or whether tomorrow it was his or Shaw's or Tyson's. Let them die, he prayed,
shamefully; let them die, but please God let me live."
(*Birdsong* is an acclaimed novel by Sebastian Faulks about a soldier's experiences in France before and during the Great War.)

Source H **Forgotten Voices of the Great War,**
Max Arthur, Ebury Press, 2004

Sergeant Stefan Westmann – 29th Division, German Army

"We got orders to storm the French position. We got in and I saw my comrades start falling to the right and to the left of me. But then I was confronted by a French corporal with his bayonet to the ready, just as I had mine. I felt the fear of death in that fraction of a second when I realised that he was after my life, exactly as I was after his. But I was quicker than he was. I pushed his rifle away and ran my bayonet through his chest. He fell, putting his hand on the place where I had hit him, and then I thrust again. Blood came out of his mouth and he died."

The areas around the front-line trenches were completely devastated by the constant shellings; in the background of this phto you can just make out the ruins of a village.

The infamous Douglas Haig assumed command of the BEF on 19 December 1915.

102

Why is the Battle of the Somme so well known?

The Battle of the Somme has become famous because of the huge numbers of men lost – particularly by the British – during this battle. The British commanders preceded the battle with a week-long bombardment, leading up to the day of attack which was set for 1 July 1916. The belief was that the artillery shelling would be so overwhelming that no German troops could possibly survive, and the British could simply walk across No Man's Land and easily capture the enemy lines.

Three terrible errors...

However, for three main reasons this was not the case. Firstly, numerous deep dugouts and shelters in the enemy lines easily protected the Germans from shelling. British Generals either did not know about these, or chose to ignore the fact that shellfire would not really damage these dugouts at all. Secondly, many shells simply failed to explode, and those designed to cut all the barbed wire protecting the Germans lines just weren't up to the job. Finally, the German forces had learned from previous British tactics: major bombardments usually ended just before the British troops went over the top, so, when the week-long shelling stopped, the Germans rushed from their shelters, put their machine guns in position and were ready and waiting.

When British soldiers went over the top – many of whom were those who had volunteered in 1914 and 1915 to form the New Army, and had never faced real battle before – they met fierce resistance from the German troops and their battery of machine guns. On the first day of the battle alone, Britain lost 60,000 men: wounded, captured or killed (see Source A).

One million casualties...

During the next five months, fresh attacks were continually launched both by the British, aiming to capture their original objectives, and by the Germans, who were determined to recapture any lost ground. The result was limited success for either side. By the end of the battle, in November 1916, more than 1 million casualties had been suffered on both sides and the Allies had advanced their front lines just five miles.

The Battle of the Somme, in 1916, has gone down in British history as a military disaster.

- What happened?
- Whose fault was it?

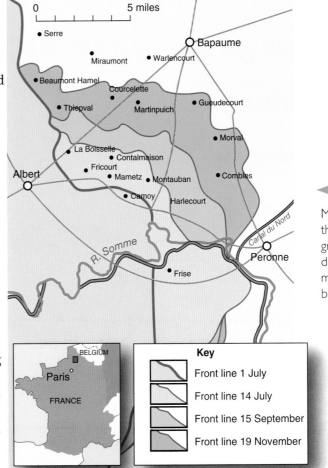

Map showing the limited ground captured during the months of the battle.

Key
- Front line 1 July
- Front line 14 July
- Front line 15 September
- Front line 19 November

Source A — The Great War,
Correli Barnett, BBC Books, 2003

"At 7:30am on 1st July 1916, 14 British divisions climbed out of their trenches along an 18 mile front north of the Somme and marched slowly forward, each man carrying 66 pounds of kit, in wave after wave of extended lines, steadily on towards the German defences. They expected to find the enemy barbed wire, trench systems, artillery and defenders all annihilated by the week long preliminary bombardment by 1,350 guns. Instead they were massacred by German artillery and machine guns, first as they plodded across 'no man's land' and then as they bunched to struggle through such gaps as existed in the often uncut barbed wire. By the end of the day no fewer than 57,000 men had fallen, 19,000 of them killed, and without gaining a lodgement in the German defences, except on the right of the line next to the five French divisions also taking part in the offensive."

Haig

The leader of the British forces at the Battle of the Somme was Field Marshall Haig. Historians have debated for many years whether Haig was solely to blame for the appalling losses. He had served in the Boer Wars (1899–1902) and many other military campaigns, but this war required very different strategies and tactics. He certainly misjudged the effectiveness of the early bombardments to German defences and then continued to send wave after wave of British soldiers to their deaths, for little territorial gain.

However, his actions must be put into the context of the time, when few if any Generals had any experience of the war they found themselves fighting. As a result almost every army was having to rethink its tactics, trying to find a way of launching successful attacks against trenches, machine guns and artillery. Was Haig therefore any worse than many others who were in a similar position of command?

A portrait of Haig, now a much debated figure in British history.

Discussion POINT ?

What qualities should a leader have?

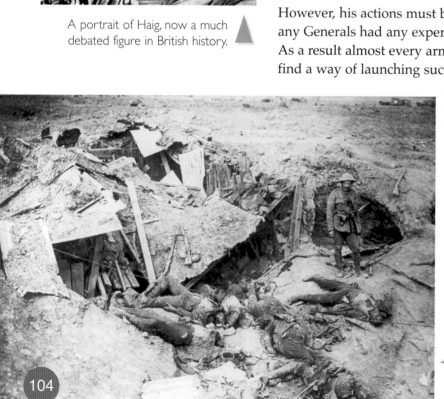

The results of an artillery bombardment: a British soldier amid the destruction around a German dug out.

Innovation?

The Great War is sometimes portrayed as being a war of innovation in weaponry. Certainly, new weapons were introduced, but many of them were not fully developed and their true potential would not be realised until used in much later conflicts (see Source A).

Source A — World War I,
H.P. Willmott, DK Publishing, 2007

"The one thing the First World War did not do was to transform the hardware with which war was fought. The war was larger in scale than any before it, but for most of its duration conventional warships, artillery, machine guns, rifles and horses dominated combat. Aircraft were in their infancy; submarines were used sparingly, as were tanks, the one major new invention for land warfare. The potential of these new weapons would not be realized until the next war.

Weapons play a crucial role in the outcome of war. Their use can bring both victory and inflict great suffering.

● What weapons were used during the Great War?
● What effects did they have?

Gas

One particularly deadly new weapon was poison gas. During the course of the war the Germans got through 68,000 tons of gas and the British 51,000 tons. Different types of poison gas were used at different times. It could either be blown by the wind towards the enemy or fired at them in shells.

Despite the formidable reputation of how gas was used in World War I, only about 10% of all who were gassed died from their injuries. However, many men suffered from the effects for the rest of their lives.

Gas actually only accounted for around 4% of all combat deaths in World War I. In comparison, artillery fire accounted for between 60 and 70%.

To do task 1
Comprehension

1. How many tons of gas in total did the British and Germans get through in World War I?
2. What were the early gas masks made from?
3. When did the tank make its first appearance?

Source B

Last Post, Max Arthur, Phoenix, 2006

"I experienced gas twice – and it's still with me now. The first time was Mustard gas, and the second lot, I only got a whiff of it – goodness knows what it was. If you got a proper dose you wouldn't be alive, but as it reached us, blow my boots if the wind didn't change and it blew right back over no-man's land – right back on the Germans."

The first gas masks were made from very basic materials! ▼

Gas masks

Gas masks had to be designed and manufactured quickly as this deadly new weapon was not expected. The first gas masks ranged from cotton pads soaked in urine to cotton pads impregnated with bicarbonate of soda. It was only in 1917 that standard issue gas masks (box respirators) were available to British troops, with a charcoal filter and chemicals that would neutralise the gas.

Tanks

The first tanks made an appearance at the Battle of the Somme in September 1916. These cumbersome new weapons managed a top speed of 0.5mph and took four men to steer them.

Tanks seen moving up from reserve positions for an attack. ▼

Source C — **Tanks,** *Simon Adams, DK Publishing, 2004*

"The British invented tank was a major mechanical innovation of the war. British tanks first saw action in September 1916, but these early tanks were not very reliable. It was not until November 1917, at the Battle of Cambrai, that their full potential was realized. At Cambrai, the German defences were so strong that an artillery bombardment would have destroyed the ground and made it impossible for the infantry to cross. Instead, fleets of tanks flattened barbed wire, crossed enemy trenches, and acted as shields for the advancing infantry. Tanks played a vital role in the allied advances throughout 1918."

Some military leaders were impressed with the potential of the tank, but life for the troops who were driving and operating them was tough (see Source D).

Source D

Forgotten Voices of the Great War,
Max Arthur, Ebury Press, 2004

"Inside it got hotter and hotter, as the only ventilation was for the engine and not the crew. If you wanted to see outside you had to look through a steel periscope which gave everything a sort of distorting, translucent glow. Inside, it was hot and steamy and steeped in a Stygian gloom."

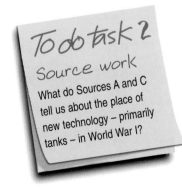

To do task 2
Source work
What do Sources A and C tell us about the place of new technology – primarily tanks – in World War I?

Overall, the effectiveness of tanks in the Great War is debatable. Although they did have a shock value and in some cases instilled fear into German defenders, in military terms tanks alone were not the war-winning solution to the stalemate of trench warfare.

Grenades

One of the most effective weapons of the war was the grenade. This small bomb gave the front-line soldier a good deal of destructive power. German grenades were better developed than British ones and were used more extensively during the early stages of the war. (For more information on grenades see Source F.)

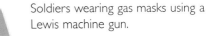

British (left) and German (right) grenades.

Machine guns

Machine guns were deadly because of the speed at which they could fire bullets. They were a vital part of the weaponry used by both sides in the war, and were one reason why attacking enemy trenches was such a difficult job with usually little success and heavy casualties. A well-placed machine gun could mow down lines of advancing troops in minutes. Early machine guns, such as the Maxim, used by all sides, were heavy and needed two or three men to operate them. As the war progressed, the British developed the Lewis gun, which could be carried and fired by just one man. The Germans developed the Schmeisser machine pistol, which was the first one-man sub-machine gun.

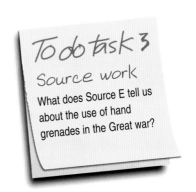

Soldiers wearing gas masks using a Lewis machine gun.

Artillery

Artillery guns fired explosive shells across No Man's Land, into enemy trenches and even longer range targets such as supply areas behind the lines. The results were devastating – the shells left huge craters in the landscape or exploded in the air, scattering shrapnel (deadly shards of steel).

Source E **World War I,**
H.P. Willmott, DK Publishing, 2007

"The grenade – a hand thrown bomb detonated by impact or a time fuse – was only widely issued to German forces in 1914. The British had almost none until Spring 1915, and their first Mills Mark II grenades often exploded in the hand of the thrower. It was not until 1916, with the Mark III, that such accidents were reduced to 1 in 20,000. … Grenades became so important that orders for their supply were given priority over those for rifle ammunition."

To do task 3
Source work
What does Source E tell us about the use of hand grenades in the Great war?

Artillery such as this one seen just after firing was used to devastating effect in the war. This gun is positioned well behind the front lines: how can you tell?

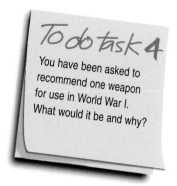

To do task 4

You have been asked to recommend one weapon for use in World War I. What would it be and why?

Discussion POINT ?

Should soldiers be made to fight if they have shellshock?

A soldier suffering from shell-shock.

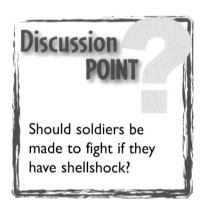

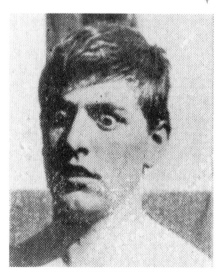

Stop the Clock

American troops arrived on the Western Front in May 1917.

Injuries

Many soldiers suffered terrible injuries during the Great War, both physical and psychological. Poison gases could cause burning, choking, lung damage, blindness and, of course, death. Shrapnel could rip open bodies and sever limbs. Machine guns and artillery could inflict injury on a scale never witnessed before.

With so many wounded, armies set up systems to quickly assess the severity of injuries and then dispatch patients to first aid, base hospitals or convalescent hospitals back home. The prime aim was to get soldiers well enough to return to the fighting. More than 75% of wounded British soldiers were sent back to fight.

British Soldiers about to enter the protection of a deep dug-out: note the destruction of the wood all around them.

Soldiers in the Great War had their endurance tested to and beyond human limits. Conditions in the trenches, both at the front line and behind, caused massive stress. Continual shelling, exhaustion, exposure to extreme danger, witnessing death and frequently appalling injury often took its toll on soldiers' minds. Mental illness was not properly understood or recognised. Over 300 British soldiers who suffered from what we now call 'shellshock' – or some sort of nervous breakdown – were accused of cowardice, court-martialled and shot. In total there were 80,000 instances of shellshock suffered by British troops alone during World War I. Little was known about the illness at this time. Today, however, it is treated as a genuine medical condition and is usually called post-traumatic stress disorder.

Source F

The Great War, *Correli Barnett, BBC Books, 2003*

"It was in the very nature of a Great War battlefield that there lay the heart of the conundrum. The defence was so strong that only massed artillery could blast a path through it for infantry. Yet it was this same artillery that created the wilderness that impeded all forward movement. As a result, advances were necessarily so slow and deliberate that the enemy always had time to bring up reserves and seal off an initial breach."

The forgotten miners

Many people still visit the Ypres Salient in Belgium to view the trenches and battlefields of the Great War. However, few realise that below the battlefields is a vast network of tunnels, shelters and mine shafts that were dug out by dedicated tunnellers. These miners – or 'clay kickers' – fought their battles underground, risking death under tons of earth rather than machine guns and shells above ground.

Why were miners needed?

As war in the trenches reached a stalemate, with neither side making significant advances, people looked for other ways of penetrating enemy defences. Blowing up enemy trenches from underneath, although extremely dangerous, seemed one way to attack German lines without the huge loss of life that was often involved in 'going over the top'.

Where did they come from?

The task of mining under the trenches was highly dangerous, and was often undertaken by the Royal Engineers or ex-miners. The main man behind the British plan was John Norton-Griffiths. German and French armies also had similar specialist tunnelling units (see Source A).

The war that took place underneath the trenches is often forgotten.

- **What was the underground war?**
- **What impact did it have?**

Source A

Beneath Flanders Fields,
Peter Barton, Peter Doyle and Johan Vandewalle,
History Press, 2006

"Norton-Griffiths' military mining career originated in a sewer. In 1910 his company had worked a part of the London Southern low level sewer contract, and in October 1913 they served another tunnelling project, a section of the Manchester main drainage system, and their work continued through 1914. Both projects entailed driving tunnels through the thick layers of clay subsoil that lie beneath the streets of each city; although Norton-Griffiths was not to know it at the time, these conditions were a reasonable simulation, and in the case of London, an almost exact match of the clay soils later to be encountered in Flanders."

The methods

Very little training was given and the miners had to rely on ingenuity to work out the most suitable mining methods. The tunnellers worked in terrible conditions, enduring flooding, extreme cold and poor light (usually using only a candle to see).

An artist's impression of mining hero, Norton-Griffiths.

To do task 1

Get imagining...

What do you think it would have been like to have to tunnel under the battlefields of the Great War? Use Source B as the basis for the end of a story about mining at La Boiselle. You must supply the beginning of the story.

Work had to be carried out as quietly as possible to avoid detection. Many rudimentary listening devices were developed to detect enemy miners, including a stick which was held between the teeth to feel for any vibrations. There was always a high risk of tunnels and shafts collapsing, and of course coming across the enemy mining towards you.

The impact

The remains of a mining project can be seen at the Lochnagar Crater near La Boiselle, France. This 200ft-wide crater marks where a mine was built, and charged with around 90,000lbs of high explosives. The remaining crater is visited by 75,000 people touring the area every year.

Another spectacular example of the success of mines came during the Battle of Messines in 1917. A huge mining operation had allowed 19 large mines to be placed directly under the German trenches. In total, the mines contained a neat 100,000 tons of high explosives. The effect of their combined explosions was huge and devastating (see Source B).

Source B

The explosion of the mine at La Boiselle as witnessed by a British pilot, from the Friends of Lochnagar website

"The whole earth heaved and flared, a tremendous and magnificent column rose up into the sky. There was an ear-splitting roar, drowning all the guns, flinging the machine sideways in the repercussing air. The earth column rose higher and higher to almost 4,000 feet."

The crater at La Boiselle.

Discussion POINT?

How disturbing would it be to know that somebody was trying to plant a bomb under you?

BUZZ WORDZZ

Detonation

The work of the miners was often overlooked by high ranking leaders in the army, who often had a poor understanding of the possible impact of the mines. Another issue is that mines generally took a long time to dig. Progress depended on what type of earth the mine was being dug in. Harder ground, such as chalk, might take twice as long to dig through as clay, or three times, or four times, depending on what else was going on at the time. The inconvenience factor was also enhanced because the miners had to be digging in front of the infantry. If the men above ground suddenly surged forwards, the mine became closer to the infantry than was safe. Mines were a much better tactic when their use was carefully and meticulously planned, such as the **detonation** at Messines, which was the last documented use of mining on the Western Front. This is not to say, though, that no more mines were dug but never detonated. Who knows, honestly, how many lie undetected under the soil of Flanders?

4.8 War in the air

Another new weapon

The Royal Flying Corps (RFC) was established in April 1912, so when war broke out in 1914 there was little actual understanding of how to use aircraft effectively in combat. Initially, aircraft were used for reconnaissance (observation), alongside traditional balloons. They were used to help direct artillery fire on the ground. However, as the war progressed, aircraft took on an increasingly important role in warfare, being used for attacking ground support and bombing missions.

Aircraft were a new innovation in warfare in the Great War.

- How were they used?
- What impact did they have?
- Who were the pilots?

Source A The Great War,
Correli Barnett,
BBC Books, 2003

"For the first time in history technology lifted warfare into the air. In 1914 the Royal Flying Corps had numbered 63 aircraft; in 1918 the newly created Royal Air Force numbered 22,000. It was a measure of the vast stride taken by airpower in four years."

World War I airmen.

Source B

The Royal Flying Corps,
from the Flying Museum website

"Initially, aeroplanes were used for reconnaissance. However, as the war progressed they became involved with a number of different roles including the direction of artillery fire and the strafing and bombing of enemy trenches, supply lines and artillery positions. As air supremacy became important, aeroplanes also became involved in air-to-air combat. This gave rise to the concept of 'aces' – pilots who shot down five or more enemy aircraft. The Royal Flying Corps also operated kite balloons as observation posts."

To do task 1
Comprehension
1. When was the Royal Flying Corps established?
2. What was a Zeppelin and what was it used for?
3. Who was Manfred von Richthofen?

The planes

Although aircraft were initially used for observation only, almost as soon as British and German aircraft met, their pilots were using rifles and revolvers against each other. There was soon pressure to advance design and technology so that dedicated fighter (or scout) aircraft could play a more **offensive** role in warfare. By the end of 1915, aircraft were being used on both sides to fight battles in the sky, equipped with machine guns and bombs.

One of the most famous aeroplanes in the Great War was the British *Sopwith Camel*. It was armed with two machine guns and one bomb which weighed 4.9 kilos.

The sky over the trenches of the Western Front saw frequent dog-fights, as pilots fought for the control of the skies. One such combat is as highlighted in the novel *Winged Victory* (see Source D).

Source C

Britain's Greatest Aircraft,

Robert Jackson, Pen & Sword Aviation, 2007

"*Before the armistice brought the carnage of the First World War to an end in November 1918, the formidable* Sopwith Camel *would destroy more enemy aircraft than any other Allied type. In the hands of a novice it displayed vicious characteristics that could make it a killer; but under the firm touch of a skilled pilot, who knew how to turn its vices to his own advantage, it was one of the most superb fighting machines ever built.*"

A fully restored *Sopwith Camel*.

Source D

Winged Victory, V.M. Yeates, Grub Street, 2004

"*They crossed the lines at 12:30 and almost at once found Huns in abundance. Williamson went down on a bunch and got one in a spin. Tom fired at several, diving and zooming, but they were very split arse and he did no damage. They went away east and more came up overhead, and the* Camels *were in a difficult position. … Earth and sky whirled round, round, and the machine-gun noise went. He came out in a dive westwards with full engine. A wonder he hadn't pulled the wings off. His hand eased the throttle as he looked up back at the Hun-filled sky.*"

Source E

When Heroes Die,

Sue Smart, Breedon Books, 2001

"*We were among the first people to see or hear them when they came over England. We were told at Holt that a Zeppelin was hovering over Sheringham; they had a 4.7in gun on the links there, but I believe its elevation was not great enough and its use would have meant considerable retaliation on the town. As it was, they dropped two or three small bombs, which were the first actually dropped on English soil. At about eight o'clock they came over us at Holt, and we put out all lights. The little boys in my boarding house were on the whole more excited than alarmed.*"

A contemporary illustration showing a German *Zeppelin* caught in searchlights during an attack. ▶

Airships

Airships were used by both sides to carry bombs. German *Zeppelins* were about 219 yards long and could carry 27 tons of bombs. Over 50 raids were made over British towns, killing more than 500 people. Civilians had become enemy targets in the latest development in warfare (see Source E).

The pilots

Recruitment as a pilot was via two possible routes: joining up from the outset as a pilot or transferring from the army. Regardless of the route to the cockpit, pilots' life expectancy was poor. Even if they could have managed to get out of a burning, damaged aircraft, the pilots had no parachutes. Many pilots from different countries gained a formidable reputation in the air despite such danger. Many became heroes and their national press used news of their prowess in the air to boost morale at home and among other forces. The most famous pilot of them all was the Red Baron.

Von Richthofen

The Red Baron – Manfred von Richthofen – was born in Prussia in 1892. He became Germany's most famous and successful fighter pilot in the Great War, shooting down a record 80 British, Canadian and Australian airmen. His blood-red *Fokker Triplane* became legendary and he acquired hero status among the German public, and respect among enemy pilots. He suffered a head injury in July 1917 but, despite medical advice, he returned to his flying corps. He was shot down and killed on 21 April 1918.

Manfred von Richthofen.

Source F

German Aces of World War I, from the Century of Flight website

Pilot	Victories	Pilot	Victories	Pilot	Victories
M. von Richthofen	80	Gustav Boerr	35	Karl Schaefer	30
Ernst Udet	62	Julius Buckler	35	Hermann Frommherz	29
Erich Löwenhardt	56	Eduard von Schleich	35	Walter Blume	28
Werner Voss	48	Josef Veltjens	34	Walter von Bulow	28
Fritz Rumey	45	Heinrich Bongartz	33	Fritz Roth	28
Bruno Loerzer	45	Otto Koennecke	33	Otto Bernert	27
Rudolf Berthold	44	Kurt Wolff	33	Otto Fruhner	27
Paul Bäumer	43	Emil Thuy	32	Hans Kirchstein	27
Josef Jacobs	43	Paul Billik	31	Karl Thom	27
Oswald Boelcke	40	G. Sachsenberg	31	Adolf von Tutscheck	27
Franz Büchner	40	Theo Osterkamp	31	Hurt Wusthoff	27
L. von Richthofen	40	Karl Allmenroder	30	Harald Auffahrt	26
Karl Menchkoff	39	Karl Degelow	30	Oskar von Boenigk	26
Heinrich Gonterman	39	Heinrich Kroll	30	Eduard Dostler	26
Karl Bolle	36	Josef Mai	30	Arthur Laumann	26
Max Muller	36	Ulrich Neckel	30	Hermann Goerring	22

NB

Some figures suggest that the average pilot might only expect to survive eight weeks on the front line – not 20 minutes as suggested in the history comedy 'Blackadder'.

A restored *Fokker Triplane*, of the same type used to such devastating effect by Von Richthofen.

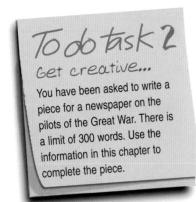

Rene Fonck

The French pilot, Rene Fonck, was the Allies' most celebrated fighter pilot, and the highest-scoring survivor. His total tally for 'kills' at the end of the war was 75, second only to the Red Baron.

The impact of aircraft on the war

Although the use of aircraft during the Great War never reached the level or effectiveness of that obtained in World War II, they played their part in this period of conflict. They became increasingly important the longer the war went on, taking on ground-attack roles and even early attempts at strategic bombing of enemy production centres far behind the front lines. World War I saw the first ever aerial bombing of civilians, conducted by German *Zeppelin* raids in 1915. These air raids increased during 1916 but gradually British air defenses improved and as a factor in the outcome of the war the *Zeppelins* had only limited impact. However, it could be argued that they had a greater effect in disrupting resources from other wartime needs, for instance at least 10,000 men were needed to man Britain's air defenses.

The idea of using aircraft in support of ground attacks was also born in World War I and ground attacks by aircraft did have a powerful psychological impact. Attempts were made from 1917 onwards to try and coordinate attacks using aircraft, artillery and troops on the ground, although it was hard to achieve because of the lack of effective communication from ground to air. 'Trench strafing', for instance, was quickly seen as a useful role for fighter aircraft and both German and French air forces developed tactics, training and formations for ground support. Germany also built specialist aircraft and by 1918 had considerable numbers of aircraft solely for the ground attack role. This importance was confirmed when the Royal Air Force (RAF) was established in 1918.

Source G From the Century of Flight website

On May 23, 1917, a fleet of 21 Gothas appeared over the English coastal town of Folkestone. On the deadliest day of bombing yet, 95 people were killed, and England began to panic. At noon on June 13, another Gotha fleet dropped bombs onto London. For the next month, the daily raids on the capital city met with little opposition from the Royal Air Force, angering the population of London. Production levels within the city dropped. Citizens felt that their government was incapable of protecting them. They demanded that the military protect them and stop the bombs. They felt exposed and helpless, just as German military strategists had hoped they would.

Unfortunately for the Germans, the effect of the bombing was not a public uprising against Parliament but a strengthening of the Royal Air Force. In July, the large unwieldy Gothas were forced to resort to night raids so the darkness could shield them from Britain's Sopwith Camels, light, manoeuvrable planes. By the war's end, the raids had stopped entirely since the hits were not worth the German aircraft losses. In total, there were 27 Gotha raids. The English reported 835 killed and 1,990 wounded. Damage from the raids totalled £3,000,000, but the loss of production time from workers having to seek shelter in the middle of the day, or suffering exhaustion from having to leave their beds to seek shelter at night, had a far greater impact.

America enters the war

Since the beginning of the war, although America was a neutral country, Britain benefitted from American finance and armaments. In 1915 an American liner, the *Lusitania*, was struck by a torpedo from a German U-boat and sank. There was an outcry in America. Many people felt that it was an unfair attack on a civilian ship, but it was another two years before America ended her neutrality and finally waged war on Germany and her allies.

In 1917, the German leader – the Kaiser – gave in to demands at home for him to allow unrestricted use of the potentially war-winning weapon available to the Germans – the submarine. Attacks on all supplies carried by ship to Britain increased and this had a devastating effect on American trade with Britain. Inevitably American ships were now at risk, and increasingly they were being sunk and American lives lost. However, it was the 'Zimmermann telegram' that finally drew them into the war (see Source A).

After four years of fierce fighting and millions of casualties, the Great War came to an end at 11:00am, 11 November 1918.

- How did it end?
- Who won?
- What was the Treaty of Versailles?

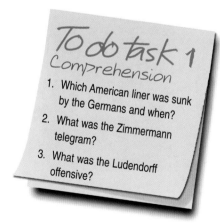

The *Lusitania* set off from New York on 1 May 1915 and was torpedoed by a German submarine on 7 May.

Source A

From the Free Dictionary website

"[German Foreign Secretary] Zimmermann sent the telegram to von Eckhardt, German ambassador to Mexico. In it he proposed that Eckhardt discuss with Mexico the recovery of their 'lost' territories of Texas, New Mexico, and Arizona in the event of US–German hostilities. He also made remarks on unrestricted submarine warfare against the USA and the possibility of inveigling Japan into an alliance with Mexico. The message was intercepted and deciphered by the British naval intelligence service of Room 40, and a copy was passed to the US Ambassador, who in turn sent it to the US State Department. President Wilson permitted it to be published 1 March 1917 and its contents caused a public outcry. Zimmermann 'resigned' shortly afterward."

To do task 1

Comprehension

1. Which American liner was sunk by the Germans and when?
2. What was the Zimmermann telegram?
3. What was the Ludendorff offensive?

To do task 2
Source work
Read Source A on page 115.
Why did America feel
threatened by Germany? Why
do you think it caused such an
uproar in America?

An American recruitment poster.

America sent an ultimatum to Germany to stop its submarine attacks. Germany's refusal led to the declaration of war. America's entry into the war meant valuable new troops of American soldiers were made available on the Western Front from 1918. Combined with the increased use of aircraft and tanks, and new tactics of attack, the end of the war was at last in sight.

The Ludendorff offensive

Germany's last big push came in spring 1918 in the form of the Ludendorff **Offensive**. This was a series of huge military attacks against the Allies on the Western Front. German leaders believed it was essential to land this victory before American troops arrived to reinforce the Allied forces. After spectacular initial successes, German forces were halted and quickly had to retreat. Exhausted, short of supplies and replacement men, the German attempt to win the war had failed. German naval troops in German ports mutinied and Royal Navy blockades of German supplies and food caused mass outrage and starvation in parts of Germany. The civilian population was exhausted and hungry, and wanted the war to end. There were mass uprisings in German cities such as Berlin. Many called for the German leader, Kaiser Wilhelm II, to abdicate.

Germany and her allies finally surrendered on 11 November 1918.

The Treaty of Versailles

The peace treaty at the end of the war was known as the Treaty of Versailles. The terms of the treaty were crippling for the losing nation. Germany was fined heavily, being forced to pay £6,600 million; the Kaiser was forced to abdicate; and the German army, airforce and navy were to be kept at a tiny size to pose no further threat to European peace. Numerous territories were also confiscated. Germany and her entire constitution were left weak and vulnerable.

The devastating terms of the treaty – and in particular Article 231, which blamed Germany totally for the outbreak of war – were part of the reason why World War II broke out 21 years later.

People celebrating the news of the end of the war.

Discussion POINT ?

What is the best way to punish a defeated nation? Territorially or economically?

The impact of the war

The Great War had far reaching implications for many people.

- What impact did it have on the world?
- What was its legacy?

The Great War is still relatively recent history, and many television and film directors have used its imagery to captivate modern audiences. But the truth is far from what is often portrayed on the big screen.

Source A

The Great War, *Correli Barnett, BBC Books, 2003*

"The memory of the Great War of 1914–18 haunts us still, even after the passing of more than eighty years, and a second world conflict that cost more than twice as many lives. Today, in novels and television dramas, the soldiers are still bidding farewell to their families in villages and back streets, shouldering their packs, and going off to the front; Edwardian society is still living out its last gracious hours before expiring under the impact of total war."

In four years of conflict, over 9 million soldiers died, 21 million were wounded and over 12 million civilians lost their lives.

Source B

Illustrated History of 20th Century Conflict, *Neil Grant, Reed, 1993*

Wartime deaths

Germany 1,770,000	Turkey 330,000
Russia 1,700,000	Bulgaria 240,000
France 1,360,000	Serbia 190,000
Austria-Hungary 1,200,000	Belgium 60,000
British Empire 910,000	United States 50,000
Italy 460,000	Portugal 13,000
Romania 450,000	Montenegro 13,000

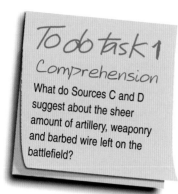

Source D

The Unknown Soldier: The Story of the Missing of the Great War,

Neil Hanson, Corgi, 2007

"At noon and four thirty in the afternoon, today and every day, the plaintive wail of warning sirens echoes over the plain of Flanders, and North East France. There is a momentary silence and then the thunderous blast of explosives as piles of munitions, newly uncovered from the former battlefields, are destroyed. There is also an annual harvest of up to a quarter of a million kilos of scrap metal – shrapnel, shell casings, spent bullets, steel helmets, barbed wire, entrenching tools, buckets, buttons and all the other detritus of trench warfare."

Other consequences of the Great War

The battlefields today

The debris of the Great War can still be found on the old battlefields. There is still a huge amount of spent artillery, unexploded shells, grenades, bombs and the relics of trench warfare, which are frequently being uncovered. Some of these items can still be dangerous, and the bombs still present a danger to farmers and members of the public, having to be dealt with professionally and safely (see Sources C and D).

Source C Today's Iron Harvest,
from the website www.flanders1917.info

"Ninety years later, the fields of Flanders continue to carry the explosives burden of that war, yielding thousands of unexploded shells on an annual basis – what's known in Belgium as the 'Iron Harvest'."

Most bombs come to the surface as farmers plough fields and the smaller ones are then stacked by the roadsides. Others emerge when road or building works commence. Farmers contact the police and the police in turn contact DOVO, the Belgian Army's bomb squad, which has a full-time unit operating in the World War I region around Ypres.

DOVO is called out more than 3,000 times every year and is almost constantly on the road in three teams of two specialist soldiers who collect the unexploded munitions and transport them to a depot near Poelkapelle. Their annual haul is in excess of 200,000 kilograms.

Every year people from all over the world visit the battlefields of France and Belgium to see where people fought and lost their lives in the Great War.

Social effects

The effects of World War I were far-reaching. The shockwaves that were caused by the war continued to reverberate around the globe for many years, and some historians believe that the way that the aftermath of the war was dealt with was one of the main causes of World War II.

After the end of the war, life in Britain would definitely never be the same again – many men would never return to their families. The fabric of society would be rocked by the loss of so many young men with much to give. The women who had stepped up and filled the roles of the absent men had finally managed to press their case for the vote, and it was eventually granted for all women over the age of 30 in 1918. This was a fitting reward for their extremely hard efforts.

Introduction

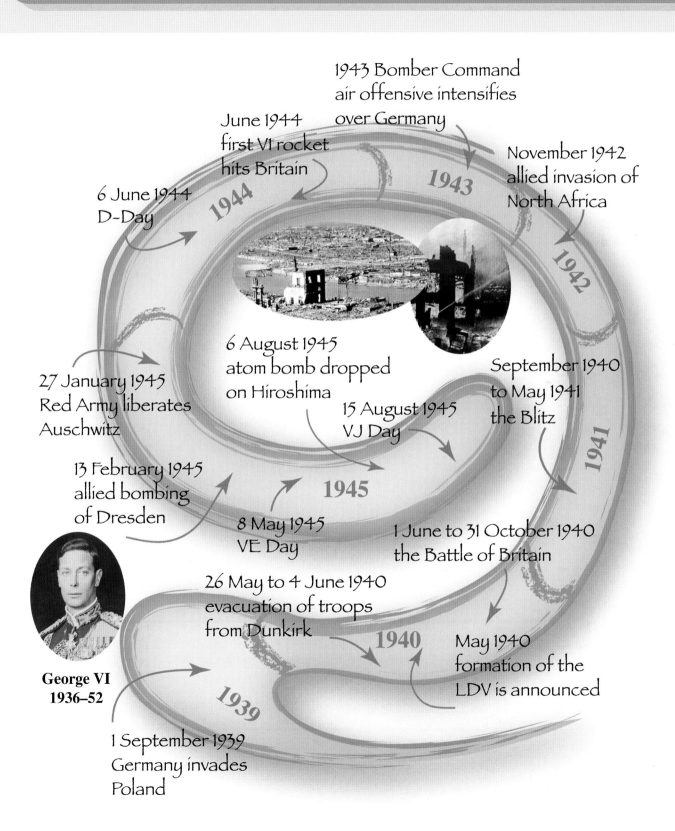

1943 Bomber Command air offensive intensifies over Germany

June 1944 first VI rocket hits Britain

6 June 1944 D-Day

1944

1943

November 1942 allied invasion of North Africa

1942

27 January 1945 Red Army liberates Auschwitz

6 August 1945 atom bomb dropped on Hiroshima

15 August 1945 VJ Day

September 1940 to May 1941 the Blitz

1941

13 February 1945 allied bombing of Dresden

1945

8 May 1945 VE Day

1 June to 31 October 1940 the Battle of Britain

26 May to 4 June 1940 evacuation of troops from Dunkirk

1940

May 1940 formation of the LDV is announced

George VI 1936–52

1939

1 September 1939 Germany invades Poland

It is June 1940: Britain stands alone as Germany, under the dictator Adolf Hitler, seizes control of most of Europe. It is World War II.

- How did World War II start?
- Who was to blame?
- Why did Hitler want to invade Britain?

Adolf Hitler photographed speaking at a Nazi party rally; he was a gifted **orator**.

To do task 1
Comprehension

1. What was 'appeasement'?
2. What were the main aims of Blitzkreig?
3. Who had the Germans conquered by June 1940?

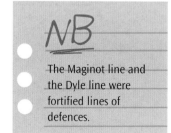

NB

The Maginot line and the Dyle line were fortified lines of defences.

An unstoppable momentum

On 1 September 1939, Germany invaded Poland. Two days later, Britain and her allies declared war on Germany. World War II had begun.

The **invasion** of Poland was the final trigger to war, but there had been a slow build-up to it for years. Some people believe the seeds of this war were sown in 1918 at the Treaty of Versailles, when Germany was so severely punished after World War I. Many Germans resented the huge debt they had to pay to the victors. When the Great Depression struck in the late 1920s, many Germans were eager to listen to the promises of a persuasive, determined leader of a growing political party – Adolf Hitler, the leader of the Nazi party.

Who was Hitler?

By 1934, Adolf Hitler was the Führer (leader) of Germany. His drive and ambition were to re-establish a strong Germany. As part of this he planned a German 'master race' throughout Europe and the world, and in doing so defied the terms of the Treaty of Versailles. He re-armed Germany, establishing a large army, navy and air force. He also took back land that had been removed from Germany's control.

Appeasement

Throughout the 1930s Hitler grew bolder, taking his soldiers into the Rhineland in 1936 and then into Austria in 1938. Next, he announced that he would take control of the Sudetenland (part of Czechoslovakia).

Britain and her allies were reluctant to confront Hitler. They wanted to avoid war and hoped that Hitler would soon be satisfied with his expansion of German lands. They followed a policy of appeasement (negotiating with Hitler in order to maintain peace). Prime Minister Neville Chamberlain visited Hitler in Munich in September 1938, and believed he had made a peaceful agreement. However, when Hitler invaded the rest of Czechoslovakia and then invaded Poland in 1939, it was obvious that Hitler was far from satisfied.

Hitler made **alliances** with Russia and Italy that secretly shared out European territories between them, and at the same time protected Germany from attack. It was a clear sign to Britain and her allies that they should re-arm and prepare for war. The time of appeasement was over.

Blitzkrieg

As Hitler's armies swept through Europe from September 1939, they used a new strategy called **Blitzkrieg** (meaning lightning war). This was a totally new form of war, unlike the stalemate trench war of 1914–18. It depended on speed, surprise and mobility. First enemy air forces were attacked using bombers and smaller *Stuka* dive bombers. Then, using high-speed tanks and mobilised infantry units, German forces would speed into the weakly defended land behind the frontline. Finally heavy artillery and regular support troops moved in to secure new territory.

This strategy was highly effective. By June 1940, the German war machine had conquered Denmark, Norway, Belgium, Holland, Luxembourg and France. The British and allied troops were beaten back towards the English Channel, until they were stranded at the coast. Germany's power seemed unbeatable. With most of Europe **conquered** and Britain apparently facing defeat, the rest of the world waited for Hitler's invasion of Britain to begin.

German troops fighting during the 1939–40 Blitzkrieg.

To do task 2
Get researching
Research Adolf Hitler and the growth of the Nazi party in more detail. How did Hitler become leader of Germany and why did he wage war?

Map of the German advance through Europe.

0 ———— 100 miles

North Sea

Groningen

ENGLAND

The Hague • HOLLAND
• Rotterdam
Breda

10–14 May 1940

Nieuport
Dunkirk
Calais • BELGIUM
Brussels ○
Lille
Arras •
Cambrai •

Antwerp
GERMANY

Gembloux

LUXEMBOURG

Sedan

FRANCE ○ Paris

English Channel

	Allied territory		Allied movements		Maginot Line
	Axis territory		Axis movements		Dyle Line

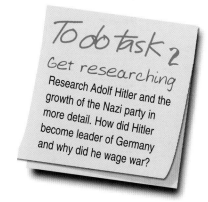

BUZZ WORDZZ

Blitzkreig
Conquered
Invasion
Orator

The evacuation of British and French troops in June 1940 has become known as the 'miracle of Dunkirk'. Why is this the case?

- Why was it important to save as many soldiers as possible?
  - Did Hitler make a huge mistake in allowing the evacuation to succeed?

Map showing the main German attacks in France and the gradual Allied retreat to Dunkirk.

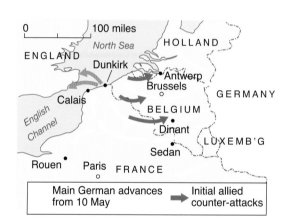

Retreat to the coast

In May and June 1940, the German armed forces used Blitzkrieg to constantly out-manoeuvre British, French and Belgian defences. Time after time the Allies had to retreat as the Germans moved fast to try and encircle and trap them. Eventually they reached the English Channel and had nowhere left to retreat to. By June the remains of the Allied armies were trapped at Dunkirk on the coast. With the Germans still advancing, more than 300,000 British troops waited for a miracle – to be rescued.

That rescue was slow in coming. Because the port of Dunkirk had been damaged and was blocked with wreckage, it was unusable by large transport ships. Britain's stranded troops were extremely **vulnerable** to the threat of the German *Stuka* dive bombers and the advancing German land forces. Britain seemed to be facing a humiliating defeat.

Why did the Germans hesitate in their attack?

Actually the German forces were exhausted after the rapid conquest of France. Supplies had not kept up with front-line troops, and the German soldiers needed time to rest and re-group. Hermann Goering was commander of the German *Luftwaffe* (the air force) and he arrogantly assumed that his air force alone could defeat the retreating allied forces. Hitler paused the ground attack, giving his armies the time they needed to re-equip. They did not try to destroy the Allies on the beaches, rather relying on the ability of German tanks to cut off their escape routes, wait until land-based re-enforcements could arrive, and watch the *Luftwaffe* destroy the Allies at will.

The British soldiers came under air attack from German fighter and bomber planes every day. Some troops felt that the RAF had not fulfilled its duty in protecting them, but in fact the RAF played a large part in ensuring that the *Luftwaffe* attacks were limited. In fact it constantly engaged German aircraft formation while flying to Dunkirk, or over the English Channel away from where the ground troops could see the evidence (see Source A).

British troops crowd the deck of their rescue ship.

Source A Spitfire: Portrait of a Legend,

Leo McKinstry, John Murray, 2008

"The RAF pilots fiercely resented the charge that they had deserted the men on the ground. Throughout the long, hard days of Dunkirk, they flew sortie after sortie, preventing the Luftwaffe *from roaming over the British lines at will."*

Operation Dynamo

With rescue almost impossible using large ships, a new plan was put into action: Operation Dynamo. Almost every type of military and civilian ship that could be found along the southern and eastern coasts of Britain sailed over to Dunkirk. The mission was simple: to rescue as many stranded troops as possible. Between 26 May and 4 June over 800 boats, including paddle steamers, fishing boats, yachts, and even rowing boats, rescued more than 300,000 British and French soldiers.

These smaller boats could get closer to the beaches to pick up troops than larger vessels. Some small boats ferried troops out to larger vessels waiting in deeper water, others simply returned back to England, with their boats packed full of troops. The smallest boat that made its way there was named *Tamzine* and was only 18ft long.

Winston Churchill, British Prime Minister from 1940–45, allowed the success of Operation Dynamo to boost the morale of the British public and forces. The newspapers and newsreels in cinemas recounted the evacuation of Dunkirk in heroic terms. There was little focus on the vast amount of ammunition, supplies, vehicles and weapons that had to be abandoned on the beaches, or the thousands of soldiers who were taken prisoner or killed.

Although Dunkirk was a defeat in military terms for the British, it was turned into a propaganda victory.

Churchill **proclaimed** Dunkirk to be 'a miracle escape' but he warned the British people of the challenges to come:

To do task 1
Comprehension
1. How many British troops were trapped at Dunkirk?
2. Why did the Germans fail to capitalise on the British problems?
3. What was Operation Dynamo?

Stop the clock

The German army arrived in France May 1940.

◄ Soldiers often had to wade out into the sea up to their necks before they could be taken on board a ship or boat.

Discussion POINT?

Why is it important to boost morale even in defeat?

123

Churchill famously said:

> "The Battle of France is over. I expect that the Battle of Britain is about to begin. Upon this battle depends the survival of Christian civilization. Let us therefore brace ourselves to our duties and so bear ourselves that if the British Empire and its Commonwealth last for a thousand years, men will say: 'this was their finest hour'."

Britain stands alone

Reluctantly Hitler made plans for the attack on Britain. Secretly he hoped this would not be necessary, and that Britain would negotiate a peace with him, allowing him to pursue other plans to expand Germany into eastern Europe. The German invasion plan was named 'Operation Sealion' and Hitler was confident that it would be a success.

In fact, the only part of Britain that was actually conquered during World War II was the Channel Islands (see Source B).

To do task 2

Source work

Read Source B. Why do you think the Channel Islands were captured by the Germans but Britain was not?

To do task 3

Get thinking...

You are preparing the plan for the invasion of Britain. What would be your priorities and what would you do to try to make the invasion a success? What would you need? How many troops would you need? Plot your ideas on a spider diagram.

BUZZ WORDZZ

Luftwaffe
Proclaimed
Vulnerable

Source B

The Voice of War,
James Owen and Guy Walters, Penguin, 2005

"The Channel Islands were the only British territory to be conquered by the Germans during the war. On 28th June, Jersey was bombed and nine people were killed. On the morning of 1st July, three copies of an ultimatum were dropped on the island threatening further raids unless white flags were displayed. The island's Bailiff, Alexander Coutanche, had little option but to await the arrival of the enemy."

The Germans invaded Jersey. How would you feel if you saw soldiers such as these wandering around your country?

A fighting spirit

In his invasion plan, Hitler aimed to get German soldiers onto British soil by 15 September 1940. Then he hoped to move troops to London and other major cities, bringing the whole of the country under his control by Christmas. The first part of the plan was for the *Luftwaffe* to defeat the RAF, and so remove the threat to German ships carrying troops across the Channel to invade. This proved far more difficult to achieve than was expected.

Churchill realised Hitler's threat to Britain and how crucial this time was. He boosted public and military morale with rousing speeches (see Source A).

The air battle raged in the skies above southern England for most of the summer and autumn of 1940, as German and British pilots fought for control and air supremacy. This period is known as the Battle of Britain, and is deemed to begin on 1 July and end on 31 October 1940.

At first it seemed that the Germans had the advantage: they had 824 fighter planes, while Britain only had about 600. Germany was training 800 new pilots a month, while Britain trained only 200. Germany also had the advantage in that it took just five minutes for its planes to cross from France, but it took 15 minutes for British planes to take off and meet the invaders, once they had been seen.

However, the balance of power was complex. The British had some crucial advantages, both with their fighter planes and in the technology available to help them fight back.

The planes

British

The main RAF fighters were the *Hurricane* (pictured below right) and *Spitfire* (pictured below left), which fought during the day, and the *Blenheim*, *Defiant* and latterly the *Beaufighter*, which fought at night. The single-seater day fighters were purpose-designed for air-to-air combat, being heavily armed, fast moving and **manoeuvrable**. The *Spitfires* were slightly faster and more agile than their German **counterpart**, the *Messerschmitt ME-109*. The *Spitfire* carried eight machine guns compared with the two machine guns and two cannons carried by the *ME-109*.

The pilots of the RAF stood firm against the might of the German *Luftwaffe*.

- Why was this so important?
- What impact did it have on the war?

Source A

Winston Churchill, 4 June 1940

"We shall fight in France, we shall fight on the seas and oceans, we shall fight with growing confidence and growing strength in the air, we shall defend our island whatever the cost may be. We shall fight on the beaches, we shall fight on the landing grounds, we shall fight in the fields and in the streets, we shall fight in the hills; we shall never surrender."

To do task 1
Comprehension

1. What was the Battle of Britain?
2. What planes were the British heavily reliant upon?
3. What advantages did radar give Britain?

The backbone of the RAF during the Battle: the *Spitfire* (left) and *Hurricane* (right).

To do task 2
Source work
What do Sources B and C
tell us about the Spitfire and
Hurricane?

Both the *Hurricane* and *Spitfire* had the excellent Rolls-Royce Merlin engine, which gave them a speed of around 350mph. They could climb quickly and were well suited to air combat. The *Hurricane* in particular was strongly built, very stable in the air and easy to repair. The *Spitfire* was a slightly harder aircraft to fly, but responded well to the demands a skilled pilot could make of it. It was also an exceptionally attractive and well-designed aircraft.

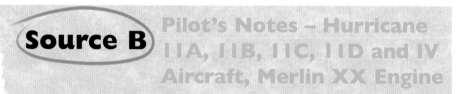

Source B Pilot's Notes – Hurricane IIA, IIB, IIC, IID and IV Aircraft, Merlin XX Engine

"'Aerobatics – the following speeds are recommended –
Loop – at least 280mph IAS
Roll – 220–250 mph IAS
Half roll off loop – at least 300mph IAS
Upward roll – 300mph IAS.'"

Source C

Britain's Greatest Aircraft, Robert Jackson, Pen & Sword Aviation, 2007

"One aspect already appreciated by RAF fighter pilots was the wisdom of arming their Spitfires and Hurricanes with eight machine guns instead or four, as had originally been intended. At first, the idea was that the eight guns would throw out a large bullet pattern, rather like the pellets from a shotgun cartridge, so that the average pilot would stand some chance of striking the enemy. But experience showed that this was a waste of hitting power and eventually the guns were harmonized so that their bullets converged 250 yards in front of the fighter's nose and then spread out again to a width of a few yards within a distance of 500 yards. In the few seconds available in which to destroy or disable an enemy aircraft, the concentration of eight guns firing 800 rounds per minute was frequently enough to knock a fatal hole in the wings, fuselage, tail or engine."

A restored example of the main German fighter used throughout World War II: the *BF 109*.

German

The main German fighter was the *BF 109* (pictured left), which was generally comparable to the *Spitfire* but was hampered by its short fuel range. Some bombers such as the *DO 17* and *He111* were becoming outdated by the early 1940s (they were derived from 1930s civil aircraft), and were only lightly armed with a relatively small bomb load. Better aircraft such as the *JU88* were used effectively by the Germans. The *JU87 Stuka* divebomber – although a key weapon in Blitzkreig tactics – was withdrawn from front line use during the Battle of Britain. It was too slow to survive against the hostile RAF fighter opposition and was really only safe when the Germans had air superiority.

Radar

The main advantage that the RAF had over the *Luftwaffe*, however, was not the aircraft but radar. Radar bases were positioned strategically around Britain's coasts, looking out to sea. They were backed up by the Royal Observer Corps (ROC) which had around 1,000 manned positions looking out for the threat from the air. They could give an early warning of any German planes coming over the Channel (see Source D).

The data they collected and the overall national picture were analysed by a team at Bentley Priory, the headquarters of RAF Fighter Command, in Harrow, London (see Source E).

Source E — **Spitfire: Portrait of a Legend,** Leo McKinstry, John Murray, 2008

"During any battle, a flood of information would pour into Bentley Priory, arriving first in the Filter Room. There it would be assessed by the filterers, who had the crucial task of analysing and organizing all the incoming reports from radar stations, the Observer Corps and RAF bases."

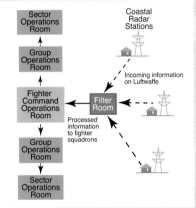

Goering's commanders correctly identified the radar stations as being a priority target: they had to be destroyed or made temporarily inoperative if the *Luftwaffe* was to have any chance of taking the RAF by surprise. Therefore they were among his first targets during the Battle.

The pilots

Pilots from RAF Fighter Command risked their lives during the Battle of Britain, flying numerous combat missions per day. Two of the best known pilots were Douglas Bader and Richard Hillary.

Douglas Bader

Douglas Bader was born in 1910 and became an ace pilot. An accident seemingly ended his career when, on 14 December 1931, he crashed the Bristol Bulldog that he was flying and had to have both legs **amputated** just below the knee. However, he re-joined the RAF at the beginning of World War II and was able to fly his plane while wearing artificial legs.

Douglas Bader (right) and two colleagues in front of a *Hurricane*.

Source D

Wartime Britain 1939–1945, Juliet Gardiner, Headline Review, 2005

"By the start of the war there were fifty-one radar stations dotted round Britain's coastline, stretching down from the Shetlands to the Isle of Wight, isolated units consisting of 350 feet high steel towers for transmission and 240ft high wooden towers for reception – both of which were impossible to camouflage. At the base was a 'receiver hut' where personnel – often members of the WAAF [Women's Auxiliary Air Force] sat intently studying the blips on a cathode ray tube."

BUZZ WORDZZ

Amputated
Counterpart
Manoeuvrable

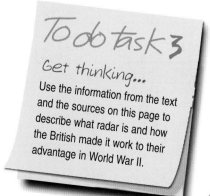

To do task 3

Get thinking...

Use the information from the text and the sources on this page to describe what radar is and how the British made it work to their advantage in World War II.

Richard Hillary

Another famous pilot was Richard Hillary. Hillary was terribly burned during combat (see Source F).

To do task 4

Get imagining...

Imagine that you are the pilot of a Spitfire or a Hurricane. You are involved in the Battle of Britain. What would your daily life be like? Use the internet or the library to find out what life was like for these pilots. Then write a short story about one of your battles in the air.

Source F — **Wartime Britain 1939–1945,** *Juliet Gardiner,* Headline Review, 2005

"*Pilots were exemplified by Richard Hillary, whose book* The Last Enemy *was a best seller when it was published in 1942, but whose face and hands were so badly burned when he was shot down that even the skill of the pioneering New Zealand Maximofacial surgeon at East Grinstead hospital, Archibald MacIndoe, could do no other than partially release Hillary's clawed hands and stretch his face back to what resembled a taut and inflexible carapace.*"

The fighting

The Luftwaffe raised its game in August 1940, attacking more frequently and intensely. On 13 August 1940, 'Eagle Day', its attention turned towards destroying RAF airfields rather than the radar stations.

As more British planes were lost, the government increased its production of planes. By the end of August, Britain was producing over 550 planes a month, while the Germans were only making about 150. Moreover, the radar system was proving effective in detecting German planes and grouping RAF fighters ready to attack. German losses steadily increased.

The relentless air battles demanded huge skill and willpower from pilots and ground-crews, who had to keep the aircraft in battle day and night, for months on end. Inevitably the pilots struggled with the reality of constant killing, whatever their nationality.

Injury and death were often only seconds away (see Sources G and H).

Source G

First Light, Geoffrey Wellum, Penguin, 2003

"What a world, Geoff, you've just killed a bloke, a fellow fighter pilot. That was just about as callous as you can get, just plain cold blooded murder. The bloke didn't even know what had hit him. On the other hand, if he had just dropped his bloody great bomb on a house, and they're not in the least discriminating these Germans, the people in that house, old, young, male or female, wouldn't have known what had hit them either. It's all bloody wrong somehow, that twentieth-century civilization should have been allowed to come to this. Just total war, I suppose. What's it all about for God's sake?"

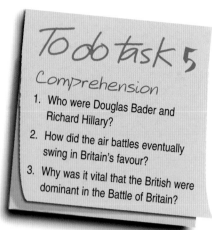

To do task 5

Comprehension

1. Who were Douglas Bader and Richard Hillary?

2. How did the air battles eventually swing in Britain's favour?

3. Why was it vital that the British were dominant in the Battle of Britain?

Stop the clock

Italy entered the war in June 1940.

Discussion POINT ?

What does it take to be a successful fighter pilot?

Source H — The Voice of War, James Owen and Guy Walters, Penguin, 2005

"Just as I rolled – too slowly – over to the left to dive away, I saw a sudden flash of tracer very close, and in the same second heard several pops, then a deafening 'Bang!' in my right ear. (I think it came from the boys above right, but it's just possible that the rear gunner of the blazing Heinkel was still firing, and if so I raise my hat yet again!) In that instant I knew they'd hit my aeroplane. A shower of blood spurted down my right side. My Hurricane was diving almost vertically, and I was surprised to see my right arm, drenched in blood, raised up in front of me against the hood. There was no feeling in it – the hand was hooked like a dead bird's claw. All this happened in a flash; but so quickly does the mind work that in the same moment I guessed at and assessed the damage and decided how to act. That 'Bang!' still echoed in my right ear, and I said aloud 'Cannon shell in right shoulder – arm may be almost severed – write that off – pull out of dive with left hand, and if necessary bale out, pulling ripcord with left hand'."

By mid-September (the deadline that Hitler had set for the invasion of Britain) it had become obvious that the Luftwaffe had not defeated the RAF. Although huge losses were inflicted on both sides, supremacy in the air was still with the British. The German air force therefore turned its focus from British air bases to London, where it began a huge bombing campaign. At the same time, the main German strategic focus turned to attack another enemy – Russia.

Winston Churchill honoured the pilots who brought victory in the Battle of Britain, saying 'Never in the field of human conflict was so much owed by so many to so few.' The Battle of Britain had been won, but the war was by

Source I — From the BBC News website

Two casualties of the Battle of Britain have been remembered in a special service 63 years to the day after they died. People from both sides of the English Channel gathered in the village of Staplehurst on Monday to remember a Belgian pilot and a local man who worked in the railway station. They were both killed when the fighter pilot's plane crashed into the station on Sunday 15 September 1940. The pilot's son and colleagues of the station ticket office clerk were at the ceremony, as were surviving pilots. The Battle of Britain, which took place in the skies over south-east England in the summer of 1940, is seen as one of the most decisive moments in World War II. About 1,700 Luftwaffe bombers and fighters were shot down in a few months while Britain lost more than 900 fighter planes. Nearly 500 Allied pilots and aircrew were killed. Among the pilots to die was Georges Doutrepont, the Belgian whose plane crashed onto Staplehurst station.

The Blitz

After the defeat in the Battle of Britain, Hitler changed strategies. Unable to subdue the RAF by day and thereby assure the right conditions for a successful invasion, the German Luftwaffe now targeted cities and industrial centres hoping to bomb Britain into surrender.

London was the first main target. For 57 consecutive nights, bombs rained down on the capital city. Then other major cities became targets too, such as Coventry, Birmingham, Manchester and Liverpool. This intense wave of bombing became known as the Blitz.

When the war finally reached the everyday people of Britain, the German bombers targeted cities.

- What was the Blitz?
- How did civilians cope?

A German *Heinkel* bomber attacks an already burnng city.

Source A

The Longest Night: Voices from the London Blitz,
Gavin Mortimer, Weidenfeld & Nicolson, 2005

"Three hundred and fifty German bombers, escorted by 600 fighters, blotted out the warm September sun as they came up the Thames estuary. They were 2 miles high and the head of the force stretched across 20 miles. At 5pm the bombs began to fall. On Woolwich Arsenal, the country's largest munitions factory, and then on the docks that proliferated along the banks of the Thames."

To do task 1

Comprehension

1. Which British city was the main target for the Blitz?
2. What was an ARP warden?
3. What was a Morrison shelter also known as and why?

Source B

The Voice of War, *James Owen and Guy Walters, Penguin, 2005*

"A little before nine o'clock the siren went again, and using the fires as beacons, the Luftwaffe sent wave after wave of bombers into the holocaust, until three o'clock next morning. Poplar, Bermondsey, West Ham and other places in the East End [of London] were bombed until they resembled desolate heaps of rubble, and at least a thousand people had been killed, many others trapped, wounded and made homeless. The planes flew up the Thames, which was lit up like a horrifying pantomime, past London Bridge, Victoria, Chelsea, dropping their deadly cargo indiscriminately. Nearby the flat, a gas main was hit, and a jet of white flame shot up into the darkness like a brightly lit geyser."

Rescue workers carry a child to safety from the rubble.

Civilian volunteers

To help local authorities deal with the chaos and **devastation** caused by the bombing, specialist staff were employed on a voluntary basis. These people were known as 'Air Raid Precaution (ARP) wardens'.

Most local ARP posts looked after about 500 civilians and there were usually six wardens at every post. ARP wardens were mainly men, with only one in six being a woman.

Volunteers were also recruited to the Fire Guard, taking responsibility for locating fires and **incendiary** bombs. These small bombs were designed solely to start fires, which could spread quickly among the tightly packed city buildings (see Source C).

The standard equipment for the Fire Guard was a stirrup pump and a bucket of sand. The stirrup pump could produce a fine spray of water which was ideal for putting out incendiary bombs. The alternative, a strong jet of water, could cause the bomb to split into pieces, thereby doing even more damage. The sand was used to deal with specialised bombs on which water would be no use.

A German incendiary bomb.

The shelters

During air-raids, civilians had to find shelter from the bombing. Sources of shelter varied depending on where you lived and personal preferences.

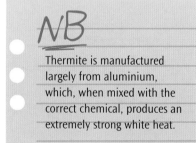

To do task 2
Get creative...
Design an advert to recruit air-raid wardens. What jobs were they needed to do and why were they so important?

NB

Thermite is manufactured largely from aluminium, which, when mixed with the correct chemical, produces an extremely strong white heat.

Source C The Longest Night: Voices from the London Blitz, Gavin Mortimer, Weidenfeld & Nicolson, 2005

"A German incendiary bomb weighed about one kilogram. It was magnesium with a thermite filling, which could be removed by unscrewing the base of the bomb. One of Tom's gang, young Teddy Turner, fancied himself as a bit of a bomb expert. He would unscrew the cap, recalls Tom, remove the phosphorous into a paper and then we'd all go and chuck it on a bonfire to see it go up."

Anderson shelters

Anderson shelters were named after the Secretary of State for Home Affairs, Sir John Anderson. The cost to buy them depended on household income, but they were provided free to those who could not afford to pay anything. They were built to accommodate four to six people and were dug into the garden. It was the responsibility of each householder to build the shelter, which was constructed primarily from corrugated sheets of steel. The shelters were designed to protect from blast damage and actually were remarkably safe, capable of withstanding pretty much anything except a direct hit. Being dug down into gardens below ground level, however, meant they could be damp and dark, and prone to flooding.

Morrison shelters

Morrison shelters were indoor shelters: 37in high, 6ft long and 4ft wide. They had mesh sides that you could see through and a strengthened steel top so that they could double-up as a table. They were built to withstand a large amount of **debris** falling on to them, but could, in doing so, also imprison their inhabitants within an inferno or a collapsed building. They soon earned the nickname 'the coffins'.

The Anderson shelter could provide protection against anything except a direct hit, as this photograph demonstrates.

A Morrison shelter, also known as a table shelter.

London Underground

For Londoners another source of shelter was the London Underground. Tube stations were not officially planned to be used as a **refuge** but, as the Blitz intensified, they were soon commandeered by the people of London (see Source D).

People sheltering in a London Underground station during an air-raid. Would you have been able to sleep like this?

Source D

The War Years, Janice Anderson, Futura, 2007

"Londoners had the Underground. At the start of the war, the Home Secretary, fearful of allowing large numbers of people to gather together and wanting to keep the Underground fully operational, refused to allow its stations to be used as shelters. Londoners had other ideas, and poured down into the tube when the sirens wailed in September 1940. At first conditions below ground were pretty squalid, but gradually improved as better lighting and sanitary facilities were installed, canteens and some 22,000 bunk beds were made available and regular cleaning was carried out. Some stations even laid on entertainment."

The bombs

During the Blitz, more than 18,800 tons of bombs were dropped on London by German forces, and 11,700 tons on other major cities. Many different types of bombs were used (see Source E).

Source E

Wartime Britain 1939–1945,

Juliet Gardiner, Headline Review, 2005

"Four–fifths of all bombs dropped during the Blitz were high explosive (HE-SC – Sprengbombe Cylindrische), or general purpose as they were known in Britain – the sort designed to cause maximum impact. They were made of thin steel to maximise the effect of the blast, and varied greatly in size. Some had a cardboard tube like an organ pipe, or an adapted bayonet scabbard attached. These, known as 'Trumpets of Jericho', emitted an eerie whistling sound as the bomb plunged to earth and were expressly designed to terrify the civilian population. The smallest and most common were the 110lb bombs, while toward the end of the scale was the 2,200lb bomb nicknamed Hermann after the portly Goering,
Commander in chief of the Luftwaffe. The 'Satan' bomb weighed nearly 4,000lb and could produce a crater that could comfortably accommodate several double decker buses. The 'Max', the largest bomb ever to fall in Britain weighed a massive 5,500lb."

V1

The sustained bombing attacks on British cities ended in spring 1941, as they had failed to bring about Britain's surrender, and Hitler's attention was by then moving away from defeating Britain and on to an attack against Russia. Later bombing attacks were launched using a development of the bomb called the V1. These unmanned flying bombs – Vergeltungswaffe Eins (or Retaliation Weapon 1) – first hit Britain in June 1944. The V1 was also called the doodlebug or a buzz bomb because of the noise that it made.

Although they were not very accurate they carried over 2,000lb of high explosives and hit their targets at over 360mph.

The V1 Flying Bomb was launched from catapult ramps, as seen here, or air-launched from beneath the wing of a German bomber.

V2

A development of the V1 was the V2. The V2 – essentially a ballistic missile carrying about 1 ton of explosives – was powered by a rocket engine, allowing it to reach heights of approximately 50 miles above the earth. It flew at over 2,000mph and dropped vertically onto the target with devastating consequences. The V2 was designed by scientist Wernher von Braun, who later went on to work with NASA on the Apollo moon rocket missions.

A preserved example of the V2 ballistic missile: there was no defence against it.

 Map showing the sites from which the V1 and V2 rockets were launched towards Britain.

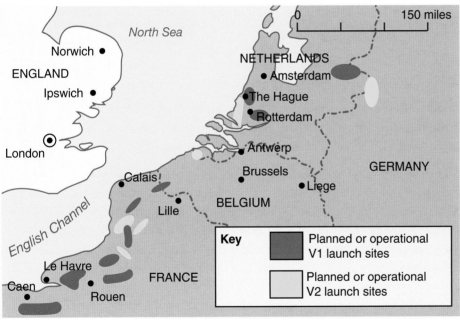

Source F

The Longest Night: Voices from the London Blitz,
Gavin Mortimer, Weidenfeld & Nicolson, 2005

"By 11th September, London's population had been sheared by the Luftwaffe. Hundreds were dead, but it was defiance not defeat that infused their blood. In Stepney somebody stepped over the corpses and the rubble and on the wall scrawled a message to Hitler: 'England forever. Keep smiling. He may get us up. But he'll never get us down.'"

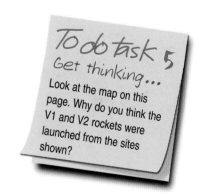

To do task 5
Get thinking...
Look at the map on this page. Why do you think the V1 and V2 rockets were launched from the sites shown?

Source G

From the Discovery Channel website
The foundations of these rocket technologies were built upon German science. At the end of the Second World War, America captured rocket genius Wernher von Braun and many of his colleagues, and moved them to the US as part of Project Paper Clip. Dr von Braun masterminded the terrifying wartime V-2 rockets. Making use of von Braun's knowledge, NACA devoted more and more of its facilities, budget, and expertise to missile research in the mid- and late 1950s.

In May 1941, the Nazi, Rudolf Hess, arrives in Britain and is taken prisoner.

BUZZ WORDZZ

Debris
Devastation
Incendiary
Morale
Refuge
Sustained

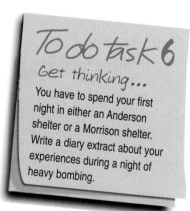

To do task 6

Get thinking...

You have to spend your first night in either an Anderson shelter or a Morrison shelter. Write a diary extract about your experiences during a night of heavy bombing.

Source H — **The Longest Night: Voices from the London Blitz,** Gavin Mortimer, Weidenfeld & Nicolson, 2005

"The sight of death was even more repellent this Sunday. At a time when ARP wardens would normally be filing into the church they were panning London's dirt looking for chunks of flesh, perhaps all that remained of someone caught by the full blast of a 1,800kg 'Satan'. Whatever was found was put in sacks or ash cans and taken to one of the improvised mortuaries where the task began of trying to identify the human flotsam."

The effects of bombing

The bombing had a massive impact on Britain's cities. Vast areas of buildings, including homes, as well as industrial centres, were devastated. More than 61,000 civilians were killed (see Sources F and H).

Many children and vulnerable people were evacuated away from the German targets – the industrial cities. Essential war industries also had to be temporarily relocated so that they would not be put out of action by the **sustained** bombing raids. As the bombs rained down upon London and then upon the other major industrial cities of England, economic and military resources had to be made available to protect these vital centres of industry and the people who lived in these areas. People had to man anti-aircraft guns; engineers and technicians were needed to work on the damaged gas lines and electricity supplies. Houses that had been destroyed had to be cleared and re-built. People often overlook the simple effects of bombs – it was not just death that impacted upon the British people. Simple, everyday ways of life were also disrupted.

However, the bombing of the towns and cities of Britain had some unexpected effects as well. Civilian **morale** on the whole remained high. The British, rose to the challenge and maintained high spirits despite the destruction and devastation. Death would never become an acceptable way of life – peoples' lives were ripped apart but life still went on.

Why was the Home Guard formed?

The aim of the Home Guard was to protect Britain in the event of a German invasion. All volunteers, the Home Guard forces learned how to man coastal and inland defences, and handle various weapons. The organisation became famous in British social history through the much-loved 1970s television comedy series 'Dad's Army'.

Most people associate the Home Guard with the successful TV series 'Dad's Army'.

- What was the Home Guard really like?
- What training did they have to resist an invasion?

Still from the BBC's 'Dad's Army'.

Source A
From the What is Dad's Army? website

"The series deals with seven main characters who live within the small seaside town of Walmington on Sea on the Kent coast. Most are 'old campaigners' from the first war, one is under conscription age, another a 'draft dodger'. All are led by a pompous bank manager, Mr George Mainwaring who gets the platoon involved in some hilarious exploits in the name of civil defence. The many disasters that befall him are not always his fault. His platoon is very loyal, and they all follow, though not without questioning, his decisions."

To do task 1

Source work

What do Sources A and B tell us about the Home Guard and how it was set up and organised?

In May 1940, Anthony Eden, Secretary of State for War, announced plans to form the Local Defence Volunteers (LDV) and encouraged men between the ages of 17 and 65 to volunteer.

The training

The LDV become known as the Home Guard. The Home Guard was composed of enthusiastic people but, at first, they were poorly equipped. Without even basic infantry weapons, some of their training had to be done with any implements they could lay their hands on, such as garden tools and broomsticks. Some units even stole old weapons from local museums! However, by the end of their training, the Home Guard was a more formidable force, that was able to throw grenades, fire machine guns, make bombs and construct road blocks.

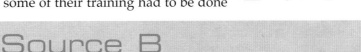

Home Guard soldiers, made up from men of all ages, being trained to use a machine gun.

Source B

Home Guard Manual, 1941
Campbell McCutcheon, History Press, 2006

"It was expected that the LDV would be composed eventually of about 175,000 men, but a quarter of a million signed up in the first twenty-four hours alone. By the end of June, with the fall of France a mere two weeks before, Britain stood alone and one and a half million men swelled the ranks of the LDV, a force that now equalled in size that of the regular army."

137

Source C

The Home Guard Manual, 1941

"Outline of training:
Enough drill to enable the men to be handled in a disciplined manner for the training purposes and in the field.
Enough weapon training for the able bodied to make them effective with the rifle or such automatic weapons as may be available.
Signalling – every guardsman is to be trained in Semaphore: specialist sections in morse.
Field-craft and elementary tactics
Map reading and reconnaissance
Field engineering (weapon pits, wiring, obstacles etc.)
First aid."

The weapons

The Home Guard had to learn how to use a large number of different types of weapons including rifles, sub-machine guns and Molotov cocktails.

NB

The Molotov cocktail was frequently used in close combat, and the Home Guard were well prepared to use it. It was so simple that you just lit a piece of cloth or rag, which had been placed in the neck of a bottle filled with petrol, threw the bottle at the target, where it exploded, hurling glass and petrol everywhere.

Source D
A Stupid Boy,
Jimmy Perry, Century, 2002

"By the time I signed on as a member of the Watford Company of the Home Guard of the Beds and Herts Regiment, it was fairly well armed with American Ross rifles that had been used by US troops in the First World War. They were very accurate and the magazine held five rounds. Thanks to the generosity of President Roosevelt, two boatloads of P14 and P17 rifles were sent to Britain."

As the threat of invasion declined during late 1940 and into 1941, it became obvious that Hitler would never make his way across the channel to Britain. Therefore the immediate need for the Home Guard declined. Even by late 1941, when Hitler was facing massive problems overcoming the might of the Russians, the Home Guard had become little more than a 'morale boosting', 'comforting' part of British life on the Home Front. Their initial purpose – to protect against German invasion – had been reduced to a defence against German paratroopers and routine patrols. The Home Guard was no longer needed by 1944, when Allied troops were making their way across Europe towards Germany. They had never faced the might of the Nazis, but had remained willing and able since their conception.

So how successful might they have been if they had actually faced the enemy? Nobody will ever know, and it is a topic that will forever be debated. Would old men, young boys and men in reserved occupations, armed with limited weaponry, have been able to compete against Hitler's finest armed forces?

To do task 2
Get thinking…
The Home Guard has been critisised since its formation. Having looked at all the information about them, do you think it would have been effective against the Germans and why?

Why did the Allies bomb Germany?

During the course of the war, American and British planes dropped almost 3 million tons of bombs onto 100 German cities. Just under 1 million German civilians were killed and 8 million were made homeless.

British leaders believed that the bombing of Germany was necessary if Britain and her allies were to win the war. The intention was to hit Germany hard wherever and whenever possible, cause maximum damage, crush the morale of the German people and disable important centres of industry. Even during the war this heavy bombing campaign was criticised by some people who thought that the extent of the bombing was unjustified. This was also the case from late 1941 onwards, as the RAF had to accept that its ideas of 'precision bombing' were found to be a largely ineffective strategy, and so 'area bombing' was adopted instead. This meant that instead of bombing specific targets, whole towns and cities were to be destroyed.

A much debated aspect of the fighting in World War II has been the RAF bombing campaign against German cities.

- Why has this caused so much controversy?
- Who was Bomber Harris?
- Were the bombings justified?

Bomber Harris

From 1942, the man who was in charge of the RAF bombing campaign was Arthur 'Bomber' Harris (pictured left). Many people saw him as **ruthless**, and he took great delight in showing house guests his aerial photographs of the targets that had been bombed. He was a fierce believer in the power of the heavy bomber to win wars, and saw it as Britain's duty to hit back with every weapon at its disposal.

Although he commanded great loyalty from his air crews, and he believed he was only interpreting the orders he had been given by the War Cabinet, there is no doubt he has become a controversial figure. Even Churchill eventually distanced himself from him (see Source A).

NB

By May 1941 it was clear that Bomber Command struggled to find and bomb a specific target, even on moonlit nights. So, by 1942, all attacks against targets were rated in terms of how many acres were destroyed. On 28 March, 30% of the port of Lübeck was destroyed, 12 aircraft were shot down and the raid judged a success.

Source A

Battlefields of the Second World War,
Richard Holmes, BBC Books, 2003

"Some of the bad press Harris has received since the war can be attributed to a very belated effort by Churchill to put political space between himself and a man with whom he had dealt so closely for three years. On 28th March 1945 … Churchill sent a draft memorandum to the Chiefs of Staff. 'It seems to me', he wrote 'that the moment has come when the question of the bombing of German cities simply for the sake of increasing the terror, though under other pretexts, should be reviewed.'"

The planes and crews

A variety of planes carried the bombs to Germany and Europe. Britain had heavy bombers such as the *Lancaster*, *Halifax* and *Stirling*, and the smaller, lighter *Mosquito*. The Americans had their own force made up from *B-24 Liberators* and, possibly most famous of all, *B-17 Flying Fortresses*.

Large numbers of air crew were required to complete the intensive bombing campaign. They were supported by bomb aimers, gunners, navigators and wireless operators, as well as the ground crews that were essential to keep the planes in the air.

A preserved example of the *B-17 Flying Fortress* bomber.

Training for the crews was strenuous and difficult. Six- or eight-hour missions were not unusual and for much of the war flying a bomber was extremely dangerous. Crews were never certain that they would return home (see Source B).

The loneliest place in an RAF heavy bomber was the rear gun turret, and the gunner occupying it was often called Tail-End Charlie.

BUZZ WORDZZ

Ruthless

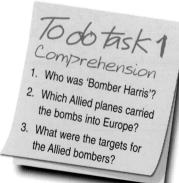

To do task 1

Comprehension

1. Who was 'Bomber Harris'?
2. Which Allied planes carried the bombs into Europe?
3. What were the targets for the Allied bombers?

To do task 2

Source work

Read Source B. What does it tell you about life in Bomber Command and what the pilots had to endure? Do you think that this is a reliable source?

Source B Luck and a Lancaster, Harry Yates, DFC, Crowood Press, 2001

"Suddenly, ahead of us in the stream, a vic formation of three planes was consumed in a prodigious burst of flame which immediately erupted outwards under the force of a secondary explosion. The leader had been hit in the bomb bay, the others were too close. No one could have survived, I knew. There was no point in looking for parachutes. I flew on straight and level, Tubby standing beside me, both of us dumbstruck by the appalling unfair swiftness and violence of it all. But there was still that deeply drawn breath of relief that somebody else, and not oneself, had run out of luck. And hard on the heels of that was a pang of guilt. One grieved for whoever was in the kites and wondered if friends might not be coming home."

The targets

Many people believe that, without the bombing raids on Germany, the war would not have been won as quickly as it was, or even at all. Others believe that the extent and power of the raids were excessive, causing far more civilian suffering and death than was necessary.

Read the sources below to decide whether the bombing of Germany was justified.

Source C

From the RAF Bomber Commmand website

"Although bombing restricted rather than wiped out German war production, it also forced the Germans on to the defensive. They had to divert nearly one million men and 55,000 artillery guns to defend the German homeland against Allied bombing. Also, German aircraft factories, which were specifically targeted by Bomber Command and the USAAF [United States Army Air Force], had to concentrate on producing fighters for defence against the bombing onslaught, instead of producing more bombers for attack. Albert Speer, Hitler's Armaments Minister, said that the bombing of Germany was 'the greatest lost battle on the German side'."

There were over 600,000 deaths in Germany through allied bombing raids through the war. Above: a *Lancaster* is loaded up for a mission. Below: effects of heavy bombing on a German city.

Source D

Bomber Boys,
Patrick Bishop, HarperPerennial, 2008

"No one who saw what Allied bombing did to Germany forgot it. A traveller in an official delegation passing through Berlin two months after the German surrender noted in his diary: 'Berlin is ghastly. I could never have believed how complete the destruction is. We covered about five miles and saw less than a dozen undamaged houses and not one in ten was anything more than a burned out shell.'"

Source E — Instructions for British Servicemen in Germany 1944, Bodleia Library

"If you come in from the West you will enter the most bombed area in Europe. Here the destruction is many times greater than anything you have seen in London, Coventry or Bristol. Compare these figures: In eleven months (September 1940–July 1941) the Germans dropped 7,500 tons of bombs on London – we dropped nearly 10,000 tons on Duisburg in two attacks between Saturday morning and Sunday morning, the 14th to 15th October 1944. In western towns from Hamburg south through the Industrial Ruhr and Rhineland – with Essen, Dusseldorf, Duisburg and many other centres, and east to Nuremburg and Munich, you will see areas that consist largely of heaps of rubble and roofless, windowless shells. Cities like Berlin and Hanover in central Germany will be no better off."

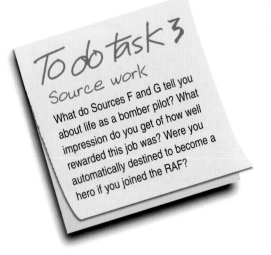

To do task 3

Source work

What do Sources F and G tell you about life as a bomber pilot? What impression do you get of how well rewarded this job was? Were you automatically destined to become a hero if you joined the RAF?

Stop the Clock

On 7 December 1941 the Japanese attack the American base at Pearl Harbor and America enters World War II.

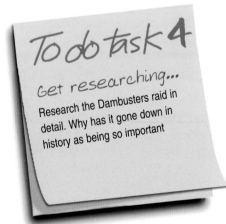

To do task 4

Get researching...

Research the Dambusters raid in detail. Why has it gone down in history as being so important

Source F

Bomber Boys, *Patrick Bishop*, HarperPerennial, 2008

"The public memory of the air war was selective. Men like Douglas Bader, Bob Stanford Tuck and 'Sailor' Malan were celebrities. They were the 'Few' and the battle that they fought [the Battle of Britain] was relatively short. The men who crewed the bombers were the 'Many' and their struggle went on and on. Of the 125,000 who passed through the fire, only Guy Gibson and Leonard Cheshire won any lasting fame. Gibson had led the Dams Raid of May 1943, a feat of dash and daring, quite unlike the demolition work which Bomber Command conducted every night. Cheshire was known not so much for damaging people as for healing them, in the homes he set up after the war."

Source G

Bomber Boys, *Patrick Bishop*, HarperPerennial, 2008

"Altogether 55,573 Bomber Command aircrew – British, Canadian, Australian, New Zealanders and others, were killed. That is out of a total of 125,000 who served. In simple terms that means 44.4% of those who flew, died. The real picture was rather grimmer. Many of those included in the overall figure were training when the war ended and never saw action. According to one study the true figure is closer to 65%."

As the German capital, Berlin was particularly heavily bombed by allied aircraft.

The Allied forces back in France

With German forces heavily involved in fighting the Russians on the Eastern Front, the Allies planned an attack on Germany's Western Front, to split the German forces and liberate areas occupied by the Germans since 1940. This attack was planned for spring 1944, when the Allied armies were to invade France across the beaches of Normandy.

Source A

Instructions for British Servicemen in France 1944, Bodleian Library

"A new BEF which includes you, is going to France. You are to assist personally in pushing the Germans out of France and back where they belong. In the process, you will meet the French, maybe not for the first time. You will also almost certainly for the first time, be seeing a country which has been subjected to German occupation for several years."

Once Normandy had been chosen as the invasion point, the Allies managed to fool the Germans into thinking that the main invasion would actually take place from Dover to Calais. This meant more German forces were concentrated there, leaving fewer to defend Normandy. The Allies also began an aerial bombing and sabotage campaign (using secret agents in France) to disrupt German communications and supplies behind the Normandy front lines.

By late May 1944 over 150,000 men were assembled in southern Britain and were prepared for the D-Day assault, which began with a massive aerial bombardment of German defences all along the Normandy coast. On 6 June 1944, almost 3,000 ships arrived off the invasion beaches. It was the largest and most powerful armada that has ever sailed. The assault was also airborne, designed to seize vital roads and bridges ready for when ground troops moved off the invasion beaches.

Films such as 'Saving Private Ryan' and 'The Longest Day' have brought D-Day to life for many people. But how realistic were these films?

- What really happened on D-Day?
- What was the impact on the men who invaded France?

To do task 1
Comprehension
1. When was D-Day?
2. Who led the Allied and British troops?
3. What unusual innovations assisted the Allied landings on D-Day?

The man in overall control of all Allied forces was Dwight Eisenhower (right). British land armies were commanded by Bernard Montgomery (left). Both men would play a vital role in ensuring a victory for the Allies.

To do task 2
Get researching...
Research Montgomery and Eisenhower in more detail. What sort of people were they? Were they good leaders?

Thousands of parachutists were dropped into France in preparation for the invasion.

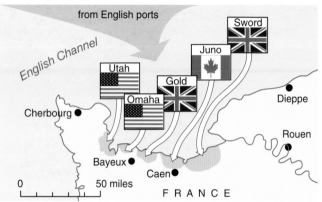

Map showing the D-Day beaches and the nationalities that landed on them.

The parachutists

As well as the British 6th Airborne Division, the American 82ndDivision and the 101st Airborne Division – called the 'Screaming Eagles' – dropped parachutists into France at the start of the invasion. Due to the fast flight in, winds over the target area and German anti-aircraft fire, the parachute drops were spread out over a wide distance. To ensure that they could identify each other in the darkness, soldiers were given tin clickers called 'crickets'. One click had to be answered by two clicks. No clicks in response meant shoot.

The troops that were the first to drop into the danger zone were given some protection by the *Lancasters* and *Flying Fortresses* flying overhead, distracting some of the enemy's fire-power. The RAF even went as far as dropping 'window' (metal, tin-foil-like strips) to confuse the German radar and rubber dummies that looked like real troops to confuse the German troops.

British and Canadian troops landed at what are known as Gold, Juno and Sword beaches. The main targets for these beaches were the towns of Caen and Bayeux, which were strategically important as they held important positions in regard to the road networks along the coast. The aim of the British and Canadian troops was to meet up with the Americans who had landed further along the coast at Utah and Omaha beaches.

On the beaches

Landing and crossing the Normandy beaches were major challenges for the invasion forces. The success of the invasion would be won or lost on the beaches. Utah and Omaha beaches were entrusted to the US troops and Gold, Juno and Sword beaches to the British and Canadian troops.

Utah

At the western end of the invasion beaches, Utah beach was the target of the American 4th Infantry Division. Having gone through the perils of a long sea crossing with high waves and many suffering from sea sickness, the troops now faced enemy fire, booby traps and barbed wire while on the run-in across the beach.

An unusual method of transport was the Sherman 'swimming tank' also known as a 'DD' tank, which floated due to a material 'skirt' that wrapped around the tank. In total 23,000 men landed on Utah beach and made progess towards their objectives.

To do task 3

Get thinking...

How would it feel to be going back to France as a British soldier, especially if you had been rescued from the beach at Dunkirk in 1940? Write a letter to your loved ones, describing how you feel; possibly a mixture of sadness at going, but hope and joy at the thought that the war might soon be over.

Source B

The Voice of War,
James Owen and Guy Walters,
Penguin, 2005

"My thinking as we approached the beach, was that if this boat didn't hurry up and get us in I would die from seasickness. This was my first encounter with this malady. Wooziness became stomach sickness and then vomiting. At this point death is not so dreadful. I used the first thing at hand – my steel helmet. I didn't care what the Germans had to offer. I wanted to get on dry land. Nothing is worse than motion sickness, except maybe 88mms and MG-42 machine guns."

Omaha

On the six-mile wide Omaha beach, also given to American forces to capture, a great danger came from the heavy shelling that rained down off the steep cliffs. The Germans had the height advantage and could shelter in the safety of their 35 pillboxes (protective structures that provide shelter for troops during attack), 85 machine-gun posts and 18 anti-tank positions.

Very little went to plan in the attack on Omaha. As the troops made their way onto the beach from their landing craft, they came under heavy machine gun and mortar fire. Whole companies of troops were killed before even getting onto dry land. Well-positioned German snipers also picked off troops and the Americans could go nowhere but forwards towards the enemy. Many ducked into the sea to try and avoid the fire but were still hit by bullets ripping through the water.

Source C

Voices from D-Day, Jonathan Bastable, David & Charles, 2007

"We could see that we were in for a pretty hot reception, for already exploding spouts of water were appearing all around us. We received one hit on the stern of the craft which wounded a few of the troops before we got ashore. Perhaps it was that first hit that altered the Royal Navy craft commander's promise to land us in shallow water. When I dropped off the ramp, my Bren gun took me down like a stone, leaving me with several feet of water above my head. Only by underwater walking towards shore did I save myself from a watery grave."

Source D — The Voice of War, James Owen and Guy Walters, Penguin, 2005

"As we approached the beach the ramp was lowered. Mortar and artillery shells exploded on land and in the water. Unseen snipers concealed in the cliffs were shooting down at individuals, but most havoc was from automatic weapons. The water was turning red from the blood. Explosions from artillery gunfire, the rapid-fire from nearby MG-42s, and naval gunfire firing inland was frightening."

To do task 4
Source work
Use Sources B, C and D as the basis for a diary entry describing your experiences at the D-Day landings. What was it like and how did you feel? What was it like to see your friends falling around you? You may want to do some extra research about what it was like for the soldiers.

As bullets rained down onto the men, bodies and deserted vehicles blocked the beach. Army medics had no choice but to treat the wounded where they fell and do the best they could. After hours of heavy fighting only two small footholds had been gained on the beach. In total nearly 2,400 American soldiers died on Omaha beach.

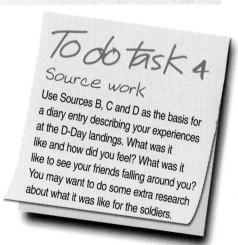

A scene from 'Saving Private Ryan', a famous film that showed a realistic view of the D-Day landings at Omaha.

Source E
Voices from D-Day, Jonathan Bastable, David & Charles, 2007

"My rifle was ripped from my hand and my helmet was twenty-five or thirty feet in front of me. When I started to jump and run, a sharp pain hit my spine from my neck to my lower back. I pulled myself by my elbows to my rifle and dragged myself into the hole the shell had made. The shell that injured me took Gillingham's chin off, except for a small piece of flesh. He tried to hold his chin in place as he ran. Bill Hawkes and I gave him his morphine shot. He stayed with him for approximately thirty minutes until he died. The entire time, he remained conscious and aware that he was dying. He groaned in pain, but was unable to speak."

The Allied ground troops were supported by the Royal Engineers, who built bridges and better roads for the troops to use. They also assembled portable 'Mulberry harbours' and piers at which to dock supply boats. Other specialised equipment available to the Allies included the Bangalore torpedo for blasting through barbed wire, the 'Crab' tank for destroying minefields and the "Double Onion", which could blast through concrete walls and bunkers.

Part of a Mulberry harbour, used as an artificial port off Normandy, shown on a cigarette card.

The cost

News of the success of the D-Day landings spread rapidly, boosting morale and bringing great hope to many in occupied Europe. It marked the beginning of the Allied repossession of Europe, as German forces were pressed from both east and west and increasingly in retreat.

Source F

Generals, Mark Urban, Faber & Faber, 2006

"The Allied landings on D-Day had been an enormous success, but for weeks they had fought foot by foot to expand their narrow beach head. The cost of this frustrating battle had been considerable: 37,000 US and nearly 25,000 British (including Canadian) casualties, before the end of June. By the same date 875,000 soldiers and 150,000 vehicles had been squeezed into a coastal strip a few miles deep."

5.8 Prisoners of war

Who were POWs?

As airmen and, later in the war, ground troops made their way into and across Europe, many were taken prisoner by Germany and her allies. A lot of them spent years in POW camps. Attempts to escape from these camps have been made famous by films such as 'The Great Escape'. POW camps existed in all warring nations, but in Japanese camps the prisoners suffered the most brutal treatment of all.

The German POW camps

There were different types of POW camp in Germany. Some were just for commissioned officers, others were specifically for escapees or punishment camps. Each camp was identified by a number and a letter. The famous Colditz Castle was known as Oflag IV C.

When a prisoner first arrived at a camp he or she would be searched and then admitted. Prisoners of war, especially RAF pilots, were not usually persecuted, except in Japan. This was because of the Geneva Convention rules for the treatment of prisoners, which the Germans largely followed but Japan, whose attacks on British and American territories in 1941 had made the war global, did not.

The following sources all come from the book *Hitler's British Slaves* by Sean Longden. What image of POW camps do they portray?

Throughout World War II, captured Allied soldiers, sailors and airmen were sent to prisoner of war (POW) camps.

- What were the camps like?
- Why is Colditz so famous?

Prisoners were housed in purpose-built POW camps, the locations of which are shown in the map.

Source A

Hitler's British Slaves,
Sean Longden, Robinson Publishing, 2007

"In the camp up to 1,000 men were housed in three vast huts where they slept in triple-tiered bunks. Conditions were so cramped there was no space for tables and chairs between the bunks. When their time came they were photographed, fingerprinted, sometimes given chest x-rays, then given a small piece of metal with their POW number stamped on it. Although oblong in shape, the prisoners always referred to this as their 'disc'."

To do task 1
Comprehension

1. What was Colditz Castle also known as?

2. In which country could POWs expect to receive the worst treatment?

3. Which special prisoners did Colditz Castle hold?

Source B

Hitler's British Slaves,
Sean Longden, Robinson Publishing, 2007

"Then came salvation. The arrival of Red Cross parcels in late 1940 changed the world for the prisoners. The food parcels, each in a cardboard box about the size of a shoebox, were designed to give supplementary food for the prisoners."

Colditz Castle was one of the most difficult POW prisons to escape from, being built at the top of a mountain.

To do task 2

Get imagining...

Source D is an extract from a biography about a man's attempts to escape from Colditz. Your task it to extend the story now that him and his friend have squeezed out of the hole. What happens to them? Do they actually manage to escape?

NB

The total estimate for Allied prisoners of war held in German prison camps is approximately 230,000, with a further 80,000 held in Japanese prison camps.

Source C

Hitler's British Slaves,
Sean Longden, Robinson Publishing, 2007

"One common feature experienced by POWs was discomfort at night. The insanitary conditions in most of the Stalags ensured they were a breeding ground for all manner of insects. POWs may have been deloused before entering the camps but the insects always seemed to reappear. The prisoners were plagued by fleas, lice, cockroaches and bed bugs, all combining to make their lives a misery."

Colditz

Colditz Castle is perhaps the most famous of all the POW prisons. It housed the 'Prominente' – in the view of the Germans, these were the important or most dangerous prisoners, many of whom had escaped from other camps.

Pat Reid was one of the few men to escape from Colditz. After various attempts, in October 1942 he was successful and reached Switzerland, where he remained for the rest of the war. In Source D he recounts one of his escape attempts.

Source D — The Colditz Story,
P.R. Reid, Phoenix, 2001

"After a tremendous struggle I succeeded in squeezing through the chimney and sailed forth naked onto the path outside. Bending down in to the flue again, I could just reach Hank's hand as he passed me up my clothes and suitcase, and then his own. I hid the kit in some bushes near the path and put on enough dark clothing to make me inconspicuous. Hank was stripped and struggling in the hole with his back towards me. I managed to grab one arm and heaved, while he was pushed from below. Inch by inch, he advanced and at the end of twenty minutes, with a last wrench, I pulled him clear. He was bruised all over and steaming with perspiration. During all that time we were at the mercy of any passer-by. What a spectacle it must have been – a naked man being squeezed through a hole in the wall like toothpaste out of a tube."

What was the Battle of the Atlantic?

The Battle of the Atlantic was fought between German U-boats and the British and American ships that brought food and oil supplies into Britain. Britain was heavily dependent upon these supplies, so an early German strategy was to sink any ships going to and from British ports.

This strategy was very successful. By July 1940 a quarter of Britain's supply ships had been sunk. The following year, less than half the amount of food that Britain needed was getting through. If the Germans could cut off supplies to Britain, they would not need to conquer them in the air or on land. Britain would be starved into surrender.

The British wartime leader Winston Churchill admitted that:

"... the only thing that ever really frightened me during the war was the U-boat peril."

- What was the U-boat peril?
- Who won the Battle of the Atlantic?

Winston Churchill inspired troops with his brilliant speeches; although he had to admit that U-boats had frightened him.

How did Britain fight back?

In the U-boat the German Navy had a powerful weapon. They were difficult to detect, and their stealth and fire-power was a devastating combination. So how could Britain disable them?

A preserved Type VII U-boat, the main submarine used in the Battle of the Atlantic.

The Enigma machines

The German Navy communicated with its U-boats at sea via coded radio messages. The machine they used to encrypt the U-boat orders was called Enigma. British intelligence experts believed that the key to defeating the U-boats ultimately lay in cracking the Enigma codes. So a huge project was set up at Bletchley Park in Buckinghamshire to try to decipher the codes. If the coded messages could be read by the Allies, then the U-boats could be targeted by British forces, and the convoys of merchant ships be kept safe from destruction.

A team of brilliant mathematicians, led by Alan Turing, worked phenomenally hard with a giant computer called the 'Bombe' until the Enigma machine codes were cracked. In time this gave supply ships a huge relief from the threat of U-boats.

A German Enigma code machine.

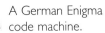

Part of the complex code-breaking machinery, the 'Bombe', at Bletchley Park.

The *Sunderland* long-range flying boat could stay airborne for up to 14 hours.

Convoys

Another strategy against U-boats was for the Allies to use warships to protect the supply ships (as shown in the illustration). The ships would travel in convey, in a tight formation, with the most vulnerable supply ships in the centre. This made it more difficult for the U-boats to attack, and exposed them to counterattack by the escorting warships.

Bomber planes

The British developed special long-range bomber planes, such as the *Sunderland* and *Liberator*. These could fly far out into the Atlantic, and escort the convoys. Radar helped them spot U-boats which could then either be attacked from the air, or by surface escorts guided to their location.

Technological advances

British technology, spurred on by the need for locating and attacking U-boats, developed a sonar technique of finding the U-boats. The system was called Asdic. It produced a sound echo through water, and could identify exactly where a U-boat was positioned. Then depth charges could be dropped to explode on or near the U-boat (as shown in the diagram on the right).

These strategies were so effective that by the end of 1943 the Allies were gaining the advantage in the battle, and some in the German navy were now referring to the U-boats as 'steel coffins'. So effective were Allied counter-measures against the German submarine threat, that, out of a total of 863 German U-boats operational during the war, 754 were sunk. The Battle of the Atlantic had been won.

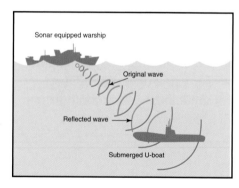

To do task 1

Get thinking...

Read the information on pages 149 and 150. Why was the Battle of the Atlantic so important and why was it so vital that the Enigma machine cracked the codes sent by the Germans? What might have happened if they had been unsuccessful?

To do task 2

Comprehension

1. Why was it so important to break the German hold over the Atlantic Ocean?
2. What was the Enigma machine?
3. What was a U-boat?

Hitler's hate list

In January 1942, leading Nazis planned the 'Final Solution' to eliminate whole groups of people from the countries Germany had conquered. They were described as enemies of the state and Hitler's list was vast. It included tramps, Gypsies, homosexuals, the sick, the mentally unstable, political opponents and at the top of the list was another group: the Jews.

The 'Final Solution' was the formal Nazi policy to exterminate the main object of Hitler's ethnic hatred: the Jews in Europe.

- Who were these people?
- What exactly was the 'Final Solution'?

Source A

Never Again: A History the Holocaust,
Martin Gilbert, HarperCollins, 2001

Pre-World War II Jewish populations

Country	Number in population	Country	Number in population
Poland	3,225,000	Latvia	93,479
Soviet Union	1,300,000	Belgium	90,000
Romania	796,000	Greece	77,000
Germany	554,000	Yugoslavia	70,000
Hungary	473,000	Italy	48,000
Czechoslovakia	356,830	Denmark	5,577
France	300,000	Estonia	4,566
Austria	181,778	Norway	1,728
Lithuania	153,743	Albania	400
Holland	139,687		
		Total	7,940,788

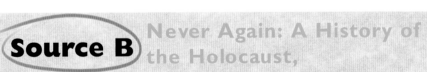

To do task 1

Comprehension

1. When did the Nazis start to plan the 'Final Solution'?

2. Over 6,000,000 Jews were killed during World War II. What does the table in Source A suggest about the proportion of the European Jewish population who were killed?

Throughout history, Jews have suffered times of discrimination, resentment and violence. At the beginning of World War II, nearly 8 million Jews were living in Europe. More than 12,000 of them had died fighting for Germany in World War I, but that counted for nothing in Nazi Germany, where radical policies were planned for their murder.

Source B

Never Again: A History of the Holocaust,
Martin Gilbert, HarperCollins, 2001

"On 20th January 1942 fifteen senior Nazis and German officials met at a secluded lakeside villa on the shore of the Wannsee, a few miles from Berlin. They had been summoned by SS General Reinhard Heydrich, who told them that he had just been appointed 'Plenipotentiary' for the preparation of the Final Solution of the European Jewish question."

How would you survive if you had to live in a ghetto the way these children did?

Source C

The Voice of War, James Owen and Guy Walters, Penguin, 2005

"Rudolf Hoess: 'The Fuhrer has ordered that the Jewish question be solved once and for all and that we, the SS, are to implement that order. The existing extermination centres in the east are not in a position to carry out the large actions which are anticipated. I have therefore earmarked Auschwitz for that purpose, both because of its good position as regards communications and because the area can be easily isolated and camouflaged.'"

As German troops occupied greater parts of Europe, more Jews and minority groups came under the control of the Nazis. Increasingly the identification and disposal of state 'enemies' became the responsibility of the SS – the Schutzstaffel – elite Nazi police and military units. Many Jews were rounded up and shot during German advances or transferred to holding areas called **ghettos**.

The ghettos

The ghettos were walled-off areas of large towns, where from as early as 1940 the Jews were being forcibly relocated, and made to live in cramped and often squalid conditions. The largest ghettos were in Warsaw, Lodz and at Lublinland. At its peak the Warsaw Ghetto held over 500,000 people, before mass deportations of its inhabitants began in 1942.

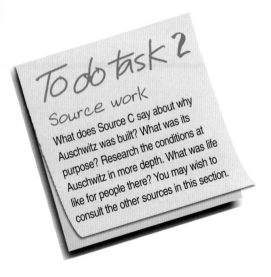

To do task 2

Source work

What does Source C say about why Auschwitz was built? What was its purpose? Research the conditions at Auschwitz in more depth. What was life like for people there? You may wish to consult the other sources in this section.

Source D

Never Again: A History of the Holocaust,

Martin Gilbert, HarperCollins, 2001

"Ghettos had existed, as Jewish quarters of towns, hundreds of years earlier. Unlike their medieval predecessors, the new ghettos were to be surrounded by barbed wire, brick walls and armed guards. The ghettos were to be located – Heydrich explained – in cities on railway junctions or along a railway 'so that future measures may be accomplished more easily'."

The camps

Many of the people persecuted by the Germans ended up in concentration or death camps. Those fit and healthy enough to work were separated on arrival at the camp and made to work in industries linked to the German war effort. Everyone else – young children, pregnant women, the elderly or sick – was put to death. Typically this was by poison gas, with other camp inmates made to burn the bodies in vast ovens.

The sheer size of the network of death camps shows the scale of the operation undertaken by the Nazis.

By the end of the war, more than 6 million people from many different groups had been murdered in these death camps. The most notorious of the camps was Auschwitz-Birkenau. All the sources included here tell the story of Auschwitz. They need no commentary.

Source E

Eyewitness Auschwitz,
Filip Muller, Ivan R. Dee, 1999

"Towards the end of the summer of 1943 a workshop for melting gold was set up in crematorium 3. It must have been unique in the way in which it obtained its supplies. Two Jewish dental technicians were transferred to Birkenau from the dental hospital in Auschwitz. Boxes of gold teeth were opened. These were teeth pulled from the jaws of Jews murdered in the gas chamber before their crematorium. The teeth were soaked for a few hours in hydrochloric acid in order to clean off remnants of flesh and bone. Then they were melted in graphite moulds with the help of a blow lamp and formed into bars."

The conditions that concentration camp victims suffered were appalling.

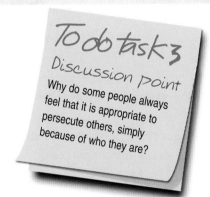

To do task 3
Discussion point
Why do some people always feel that it is appropriate to persecute others, simply because of who they are?

Source F

Eyewitness Auschwitz,
Filip Muller, Ivan R. Dee, 1999

"As soon as the Zyklon B crystals came into contact with air the deadly gas began to develop, spreading first at floor level and then rising to the ceiling. It was for this reason that the bottom layer of corpses always consisted of children as well as the old and the weak, while the tallest and strongest lay on top."

Source G

Forgotten Voices of the Holocaust, *Lyn Smith,*
Ebury Press, 2005

"Denis Avery – British prisoner of war, Buna – Monowitz, Auschwitz-Birkenau 'Now dreadful things were happening in Auschwitz-Birkenau during 1944. They were gassing and burning thousands of people who couldn't work any more because of their failing strength; I knew practically everything that was going on there. I knew that from all over the continent people would be brought to Auschwitz-Birkenau: men, women, children, old people; then they were sorted out and gassed right away. There were heaps and heaps of clothing, glasses, footwear – huge warehouses full of possessions taken from these people. They just put them into the gas chambers using this Zyklon B gas and then they were burned. And this happened day in and day out.'"

BUZZ WORDZZ

Ambitious
Ghetto

153

On 6 August 1945 the first atomic bomb was dropped.

- Why was it dropped and where?
- What was the effect?
- Was it right to use it?

A devastating moment

After the war in Europe had ended in May 1945, the war with Japan raged on. America believed that to avoid having to invade Japan and suffer heavy casualties, the time had come to use the most powerful weapon ever produced – the atomic bomb.

Source A

From the BBC On This Day website

"1945: US drops atomic bomb on Hiroshima

The first atomic bomb has been dropped by a United States aircraft on the Japanese city of Hiroshima.

President Harry S. Truman, announcing the news from the cruiser, USS Augusta, in the mid-Atlantic, said the device was more than 2,000 times more powerful than the largest bomb used to date.

An accurate assessment of the damage caused has so far been impossible due to a huge cloud of impenetrable dust covering the target. Hiroshima is one of the chief supply depots for the Japanese army.

The bomb was dropped from an American B-29 Superfortress, known as Enola Gay, at 0815 local time. The plane's crew say they saw a column of smoke rising and intense fires springing up.

The President said the atomic bomb heralded the 'harnessing of the basic power of the universe'. It also marked a victory over the Germans in the race to be first to develop a weapon using atomic energy.

President Truman went on to warn the Japanese the Allies would completely destroy their capacity to make war.

The Potsdam declaration issued 10 days ago, which called for the unconditional surrender of Japan, was a last chance for the country to avoid utter destruction, the President said.

'If they do not now accept our terms they may expect a rain of ruin from the air the like of which has never been seen on Earth. Behind this air attack will follow by sea and land forces in such number and power as they have not yet seen, but with fighting skill of which they are already aware'."

Map showing the Japanese targets at the end of World War II.

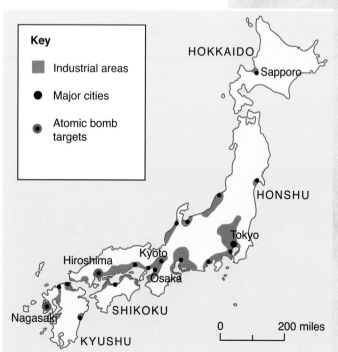

Key

- Industrial areas
- Major cities
- Atomic bomb targets

HOKKAIDO

Sapporo

HONSHU

Tokyo

Kyoto

Hiroshima

Osaka

Nagasaki

SHIKOKU

KYUSHU

0   200 miles

Source B

The Effects of the Atomic Bomb,
from the *Independent* newspaper website

"Sixty years ago, Tsunao Tsuboi was, like thousands of survivors of the world's first nuclear attack, wandering this shattered city in search of water.

'People had eyeballs dangling out of their sockets and skin hanging from bones,' he says, describing the scene as a living hell.

Hiroshima had been known as the City of Water when the bomb nicknamed Little Boy detonated in a piercing blue sky at 8.15am on 6 August 1945. It caused a searing fireball that left him burnt so badly he later fell into a month-long coma. 'When I came to, the war was over. I thought it was a trick.'

Today he is an 80-year-old man with cancer and burn scars across his body and face, but happy to be alive among the estimated 55,000 people commemorating the bomb victims in Hiroshima's Peace Memorial Park.

'Every year I come to pray that nobody else will have to experience what we did,'he says. 'I pray that the world will abandon these weapons for ever.'

A fellow survivor, or hibakusha, Isao Aratani, says he has come to pay respects to his dead schoolfriends, more than two-thirds of whom died in the explosion.

He remembers a 'thunderous boom' and being thrown to the ground by a blast of 'yellow heat'. Later he saw enraged locals beating the body of a downed US pilot that had been strapped to a bridge near the centre of the city. 'Some people continued to lash the body even after the soldier was dead.'"

The mushroom-shaped cloud now familiar with nuclear weapons, photographed over Hiroshima in August 1945.

Three days later, a second atomic bomb was dropped on Nagasaki. The following day Japan surrendered and World War II was over.

To do task 1
Comprehension
1. Why was the atom bomb used?
2. Which plane dropped the bomb on Hiroshima?
3. Which other city had an atom bomb dropped on it?

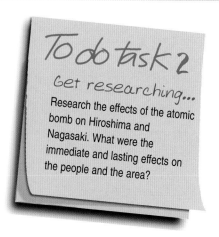

To do task 2

Get researching...

Research the effects of the atomic bomb on Hiroshima and Nagasaki. What were the immediate and lasting effects on the people and the area?

The devastation caused by atomic bombs in Japan is easily seen from these photos of Hiroshima and Nagasaki. ▼

Stop the Clock

Mussolini was killed on 28 April 1945.

Discussion POINT?

Should any nations be allowed to have nuclear weapons?

The effects

The damage caused by these bombs was devastating, and simply unlike any other destruction seen in World War II.

Source C

Hiroshima, Nagasaki, and Subsequent Weapons Testing,
from the World Nuclear Association website

"In Hiroshima, of a resident civilian population of 250,000 it was estimated that 45,000 died on the first day and a further 19,000 during the subsequent four months. In Nagasaki, out of a population of 174,000, 22,000 died on the first day and another 17,000 within four months. Unrecorded deaths of military personnel and foreign workers may have added considerably to these figures.

To the 103,000 deaths from the blast or acute radiation exposure have since been added those due to radiation induced cancers and leukaemia, which amounted to some 400 within 30 years, and which may ultimately reach about 550. (Some 93,000 exposed survivors are still being monitored.)"

Many people believed that, despite the devastating effects of the atomic bomb, it spared the lives of at least 250,000 American troops who would otherwise have had to mount a land invasion of Japan. Other people have since argued that Japan would have surrendered anyway, and the Americans were just determined to test the bombs on a real target, having invested so much money into their development.

Although World War I, 1914–18, is known as the 'Great War', World War II, as is evident from the figures in the table on page 157, was even 'greater' and more catastrophic.

Unlike the Great War, which led to the Treaty of Versailles, punishing Germany for the war and forcing them to accept crippling reparations and the infamous 'Article 231 – War Guild Clause', World War II resulted in a different form of punishment. What do the Sources D–F suggest about what happened to Germany and the leading Nazis after the war?

Death figures for World War II vary from source to source. These figures are believed to be reasonably accurate.

Country	Military	Civilian	Total
USSR	12 million	15 million	27 million
Germany	3.25 million	2.44 million	5.69 million
Japan	1.5 million	500,000	2 million
France	245,000	350,000	595,000
Great Britain	403,000	92,700	495,000

*Civilian numbers include those killed as a result of the Holocaust.
Source: www.historyonthenet.com/WW2/statistics.htm

Source D   From the BBC website

In November 1945, in the German city of Nuremberg, the victors of the World War Two began the first international war crimes trial. … Now many of the leaders of the party were on trial for their lives, only a short distance from the grand arena where they had been fêted by the German people.

The 21 defendants came from very different backgrounds. Some, like Hitler's chosen successor Hermann Goering, were senior politicians – their responsibility clear.

Others were there because senior party leaders Heinrich Himmler, head of the feared SS, and Joseph Goebbels, head of propaganda – had killed themselves rather than face capture and trial. Their deputies or juniors stood on trial instead of them. But most of them were regarded by the western public, rightly or wrongly, as key playmakers in a system that had brought war to Europe and cost the lives of 50 million people.

The charges laid at their door were extraordinary. They were collectively accused of conspiring to wage war, and committing crimes against peace, crimes against humanity (including the newly defined crime of genocide) and war crimes in the ordinary sense (abuse and murder of prisoners, killing of civilians and so on). This catalogue of sin was difficult for many of the defendants to come to terms with. …

Two prisoners in particular came to represent opposite poles in their reaction to the trials and the accusation of massive crimes. Hermann Goering, the man Hitler chose as his successor in the 1930s and the most flamboyant and ambitious of the party hierarchy, prepared to defend Hitler and the Reich's war policy rather than admit that what had been done was criminal.

On the other hand Albert Speer, the youthful architect who rose to run Germany's armaments effort during the war, accepted from the start the collective responsibility of the defendants for the crimes of which they were accused and tried to distance himself from Hitler's ghostly presence at the tribunal.

World War II is still very recent history. Unlike the Great War, there are many veterans who served in the war, and civilians who lived through it, who are alive today. This means that it is still very much in the hearts and minds of the British public, and of people worldwide. Grandparents and great grandparents are valuable and reliable sources of information on the war. Bookshops abound with tales of the 'Home Front', *Spitfires* and war-time heroes. Television channels show programmes about prisoner of war camps, and recount individual experiences of this period. The impact of the war, however, is far more wide reaching, having had an impact on international relations for many years after the end of the conflict.

To do task 3

Get thinking...

1. Make a list of how World War II still impacts upon our daily lives. How many ways can you think of? How much do they have an impact on you and your family?

2. Do you think we will ever have another global conflict?

3. Would you be willing to fight in a war?

Source E

From the Allsands website

"In 1945, just after World War II, the alliance between the United States, Britain and the USSR ended. An intense rivalry between communist and non-communist nations led to the Cold War. It's called the Cold War because it never led to armed or 'hot' conflict. At the end of World War II, at the Yalta Conference, Germany was divided into four occupied zones controlled by Great Britain, France, the Soviet Union, and the United States. Berlin was also divided into four sections. Lack of a mutual agreement on German re-unification marked the start of the Cold War. When the USA decided to drop the atomic bomb on Japan, the USSR was upset that America had secretly developed the bomb."

Source F

from the Schoolnet website

"British and USA troops were advancing from the west and the Red Army from the east. At the Yalta conference it was agreed to divide Germany up amongst the Allies. However, all parties to that agreement were aware that the country that actually took control of Germany would be in the strongest position over the future of this territory.

The main objective of Winston Churchill and Stalin was the capture of Berlin, the capital of Germany. Franklin D. Roosevelt did not agree and the decision of the USA Military commander, General Dwight Eisenhower, to head south-east to Dresden, ensured that Soviet forces would be the first to reach Berlin."

The threat of a world conflict still hangs over all nations. Who is to say that it may never occur? Numerous organisations exist across the world that seek to preserve world peace. The United Nations is one such organisation, established to do just that.

Source G

The United Nations,
from the Directgov website

"The United Nations (UN) is an international organisation created in 1945, after the end of World War II. The UK and 50 other countries signed the UN Charter – a commitment to preserve peace through international co-operation. Nearly every nation in the world now belongs to the UN, with 192 member countries."

Societies and individuals must all work hard to ensure that conflict occurs as infrequently as possible. Learning about, and remembering the lessons of the past, will contribute to this, for we all must learn from the mistakes other people have made, and try to avoid them in the future.

Abdicate – renounce the throne or position as emperor

Administration – another word for 'management'

Alliances – established connections, often military

Ambitious – hoping to get on in life

Amputated – removed by cutting off

Anglican – Church of England

Appalling – terrible

Apparent – obvious

Armada – fleet of ships

Artillery – heavy guns

Assassinated – killed

Bailey – main living area in a motte and bailey castle

Battalion – a grouping of men in an army

Blitzkreig – lightning war strategy used by Hitler

Blockaded – cut off forcibly

Campaigner – one who launches campaigns

Castellan – a man in charge of castle defences

Catholicism – the Catholic religion. The Pope is head of the Catholic Church

Cavalry – men on horseback

Claim – right to

Conquered – overtaken by force

Conscription – forced recruitment to the armed forces

Conscientious – thinking in terms of right or wrong

Contender – contestant

Counterpart – similar, closely resembling

Crescent – a curved shape

Crowned – made king or queen

Deadlock – stalemate

Debris – rubble

Detonation – explosion

Devastation – terrible destruction

Embarkation – get on/onboard

Execution – killing

Expansionist – concerned with expanding/making bigger

Extravagant – in excess

Formidable – dangerous/hard to beat

Fyrd – non-professional Anglo Saxon soldiers

Galleons – ships

Ghetto – an area of a city, walled off, for certain races of people

Housescarl – professional English soldier – usually armed with a two-handed battle axe

Illegitimate – not legal

Imperial – connected to the Empire

Incendiary – causing/able to cause fire

Innovation – creating new products

Invasion – entering by force

Latrine – toilet

Luftwaffe – the German air force

Maiming – wounding terribly

Manoeuvrable – easily moved

Mantlet – shield

Mercenaries – paid soldiers

Morale – confidence/feeling of well being

Munitions – armaments

Mutilating – disfiguring

Offensive – attacking

Orator – someone who speaks well

Palisade – defensive wooden fence

Parliament – representative body

Patriotism – loyalty to your country

Perilous – dangerous

Plunder – illegally gained property

Portcullis – a heavy metal gate blocking the way into a castle

Priority – order of importance

Proclaimed – announced

Propaganda – promotional information, often overly exaggerated

Protestant – member of a branch of Christianity established during the Reformation

Quarrel – crossbow bolt/argument

Radical - revolutionary

Rationed – restricted/shared out

Recruitment – encouraging people to join up

Refuge – shelter

Registration – signing up

Rendezvous – meeting up

Resistance – opposition

Revolutionary – against normal thinking/actions

Rigging – sails/ropes

Rousing – short for arousing/getting interest in

Ruthless – without compassion

Scurvy – disease caused by a lack of vitamin C in the diet

Stranglehold – unbreakable power

Strategic – to do with strategy/planning

Superior – better than

Supremacy – overall control or domination

Surveillance – looking out over/watching

Sustained – continuous

Tankard – large mug from which ale or beer is drunk

Telegrams – messages sent by the technology of 'telegraph'

Territories – lands

Tribunals – military/employment courts

Vulnerable – needing protection

Acknowledgements

Chapter 1 photo acknowledgements: p.7 top and bottom – iStock, middle C. Tait / Ancient Art & Architecture Collection Ltd; p.16 with special authorisation of the city of Bayeux Giraudon / The Bridgeman Art Library; p.19 top iStock, middle The British Library / HIP, bottom The Print Collector / Alamy; p.21 top iStock, bottom The Print Collector / HIP; p.22 top Franco Tiné / Fotolia, bottom Royal Armouries Museum; p.25 Museum of London / HIP; p.26 iStock; p.30 iStock; p.31 iStock; p.33 top and bottom iStock; p.36 Hulton Archive / Getty; p.45 Robert Estall Photo Agency / Alamy.

Chapter 2 photo acknowledgements: p.47 Mary Evans Picture Library; p.49 iStock; p.51 top PA Photos, bottom Terry Fincher, Photo Int. / Alamy; p.52 top iStock, bottom Mary Evans Picture Library; p.53 iStock; p.56 The Print Collector / Alamy; p.57 Mary Evans Picture Library; p.58 Getty Images / Hulton Archive; p.59 top iStock, bottom Fotolia; p.60 top Lambeth Palace Library, London, UK / The Bridgeman Art Library, middle and bottom Mary Evans Picture Library; p.62 Mary Evans Picture Library; p.63 top Mary Evans Picture Library, bottom iStock.

Chapter 3 photo acknowledgements: p.68 iStock; p.69 UPPA / Photoshot; p.70 iStock; p.71 UPPA / Photoshot; p.74 iStock; p.75 Mary Evans Picture Library / Alamy; p.77 iStock; p.81 top and bottom Mary Evans Picture Library; p.83 top Illustrated London News Ltd / Alamy, bottom National Army Museum, London / The Bridgeman Art Library; p.84 Fotolia; p.85 top Private Collection / The Bridgeman Art Library, bottom Museum of London.

Chapter 4 photo acknowledgements: p.89 top INTERFOTO Pressebildagentur / Alamy, bottom The Granger Collection New York / Topfoto; p.90 Hulton-Deutsch Collection / CORBIS; p.91 Robert and Tony Robinson; p.92 top left Getty, top right iStock, bottom Mary Evans Picture Library / Alamy; p.93 Mansell / Time & Life Pictures / Getty Images; p.94 Imperial War Museum; p.96 Ronald Grant Archive / Columbia Pictures, p.98 [new photo]; p.100 Wellcome Library, London, Wellcome Images; p.101 UPPA / Photoshot; p.102 top and bottom Imperial War Museum; p.104 top and bottom UPPA / Photoshot; p.106 top UPPA / Photoshot, bottom akg-images / Alamy; p.107 top and middle UPPA / Photoshot, bottom Wellcome Library, London, Wellcome Images; p.108 Mary Evans Picture Library / Alamy; p.110 Norman Price / Alamy; p.111 Imperial War Museum; p.112 top Jetpics / Photolia, bottom The Print Collector / Alamy; p.113 top UPPA / Photoshot, bottom Stano Novak / Photolia; p.114 Corbis; p.115 Mary Evans Picture Library; p.116 top INTERFOTO Pressebildagentur / Alamy, bottom UPPA / Photoshot; p.117 danieldefotograaf / Fotolia.

Chapter 5 photo acknowledgements: p.120 UPPA / Photoshot; p.121 Heinrich Hoffmann / Time & Life Pictures / Getty Images; p.122 Imperial War Museum; p.123 UPPA / Photoshot; p.124 UPPA / Photoshot; p.125 left iStock, right Graham Taylor / Fotolia; p.126 Thomas Wagner / Fotolia; p.127 UPPA / Photoshot; p.131 INTERFOTO Pressebildagentur / Alamy; p.132 top and bottom INTERFOTO Pressebildagentur / Alamy; p.132 top and middle UPPA / Photoshot, bottom Popperfoto / Getty Images; p.133 iStock; p.134 nebucadnezzar / Fotolia; p.136 UPPA / Photoshot; p.137 top STARSTOCK / Photoshot, bottom Trinity Mirror / Mirrorpix / Alamy; p.138 UPPA / Photoshot; p.139 UPPA / Photoshot; p.140 top and bottom iStock; p.141 top and bottom UPPA / Photoshot; p.142 UPPA / Photoshot; p.143 left Newscom / Photoshot, right UPPA / Photoshot; p.144 Hulton-Deutsch Collection / CORBIS; p.145 Bandphoto Agency / Photoshot; p.146 UPPA / Photoshot; p.148 iStock; p.149 top Imperial War Museum, middle left iStock, middle right : Starstock / Photoshot, bottom UPPA / Photoshot; p.150 Alamy; p.152 top akg-images, bottom The Wiener Library London; p.153 top Mary Evans Picture Library / Alamy, bottom UPPA / Photoshot; p.155 UPPA / Photoshot; p.156 top and bottom UPPA / Photoshot.